ECHOES
of Time

ALSO BY JOSEPH COLWELL

Canyon Breezes:
Exploring Magical Places in Nature

Zephyr of Time:
Meditations on Time and Nature

Sands of Time: A Flight of Discovery
and Search for Meanings of Time

Tales of Ravens Nest
A Life, A Place: Stories and Reflections

ECHOES
of Time

*Reflections on the Mesas and
Canyons of the Dominguez-Escalante
National Conservation Area*

JOSEPH COLWELL

Artist-in-Residence
of the Dominguez-Escalante NCA,
Bureau of Land Management

Lichen Rock Press
Hotchkiss, Colorado 81419

Editing: Katherine Colwell
Book design and publishing services: Constance King Design

Photography

Katherine Colwell: Cover photo, top; p.108 top; p.110 top & bottom; p.111 top & bottom; p.113 bottom; p.114 top & bottom.
Joseph Colwell: Front cover, bottom; back cover, top; p.108 bottom; p.109 top & bottom; p.112 top; p.113, top.
Bob Wick, BLM: Back cover, inset; p.112, bottom.
Map, p.115, courtesy of BLM.

Facing page: *Colorful guardian of the canyons*. Bob Wick, BLM.

Lichen Rock Press
Hotchkiss, Colorado
ColwellCedars.com

ISBN: 978-0-9962222-3-5
Printed in USA

CONTENTS

AUTHOR'S INVITATION

IN APRIL, 2017, I was sitting at the Potholes Picnic Area in Escalante Canyon eating lunch. I was on a tour sponsored by Delta County Tourism Cabinet and the Dominguez-Escalante National Conservation Area (NCA) of the Bureau of Land Management (BLM). We were introduced to the NCA and its recreation opportunities. While staring down into the pools and the swirling spring runoff surging through the black bedrock slot canyon, I composed an essay in my head. The black rock is the basement rock similar to that underlying the entire Colorado Plateau. Here on the Uncompahgre Plateau, it is part of the ancestral Rocky Mountains. This rock, over one billion years old, was once pushed to unknown heights, only to be eroded back to sea level, then overlain by thousands of feet of sedimentary rock that stretched for hundreds of miles in all directions and later formed the slickrock canyons and wonderlands of several states. Because it lies hidden underneath the remains of what was once a huge mountain range, uplifted once again and now reduced by erosion to a high plateau, I found it symbolic of the geologic mysteries of a huge chunk of the western United States.

I asked a representative of the Colorado Canyons Association—a partner of the BLM in serving as the interpretive arm of this area—if they would be interested in me writing a series of essays about this area. Even though I had lived within a half hour drive of the NCA for over twenty years, I had only visited the edges a few times. I knew virtually nothing about the label *National Conservation Area,* a small embarrassment since my career was with the U.S. Forest Service, a close cousin of the BLM. Collin Ewing, the NCA manager, gave a very thorough presentation of what the NCA is and the secrets it holds. I was hooked. Collin signed me up as Artist-in-Residence, a label I felt was a little intimidating since I didn't consider myself a typical artist, for example a painter or photographer.

So I hiked and drove to various places, looking and listening. I found scenery and ecosystems I was familiar with, but with a slightly different twist. Local residents, land managers and politicians decided several years ago to draw lines around this area and other nearby canyons so Congress could give them distinct labels: *National Conservation Areas*. These canyons and rivers are worthy of national park status if only they had been somewhere else. Here, they seemed common. They are not. The canyons of the Gunnison River, Escalante, Big and Little Dominguez Creeks, and a multitude of other lesser canyons are special. With much of this NCA designated official *Wilderness*, and most of it rugged and hard to get to, it maintains its primitive character, special but similar to millions of other acres across the Colorado Plateau. It is special and I wanted to capture some of its character as I pondered what was here and what it meant. I have difficulty separating the significance of time—millions of years of time—from the life that is here now. From the desert bighorn sheep on the cliffs, to the eagles flying overhead, the lizards scampering among the rocks and the sagebrush and pinyon pine dotting the mesas, this place deserves our respect and introspection.

I hope I have captured some of the awe that I find in this special place and invite you to visit and explore some of the best this world has to display. All you have to do is look and listen, and enjoy your discoveries.

I wish to thank Collin Ewing, BLM National Conservation Area Manager, for realizing this opportunity to spread the message about the little known NCA, and for taking a chance that I might be able to help with it. I also thank Rebecca Dykes, wilderness ranger, who was a tremendous help in coordinating my trips and research into the NCA with others in the BLM. She also was a patient hiking companion with this writer with aging legs. She is one of those people who has the enviable job of spending all summer hiking and driving the trails and roads of this wonderland. Kate Graham and Joe Neuhof from the Colorado Canyons Association provided words of encouragement and support. Other BLM folks who gave me good advice and guided tours included Eric Eckberg and Glade Hadden. Bruce "Rooster" Barnhart, the experienced and knowledgeable river ranger, took me on a canoe trip on the river under the magical October yellow of cottonwoods and riverside vegetation. Andres Aslan of Colorado Mesa University helped me understand the Uncompahgre geology a little better. I also relied on the wisdom and good advice of my editor and soulmate, Katherine Colwell for improving a sometimes rough collection of words and thoughts.

PREFACE

One thing only I know, and that is I know nothing.
Socrates

IN THE SPRING of 2017, I discovered the Uncompahgre Plateau and its lower eastern edges, designated by Congress as the Dominguez-Escalante National Conservation Area. This canyon wilderness, between Montrose and Grand Junction, reawakened my love affair with the Colorado Plateau slickrock canyon country. But it confused me with its added geologic intrigue. It is part of the Uncompahgre Plateau, a remnant of the ancient and long-eroded ancestral Rocky Mountains. This was a new twist and confused me with its tangled history of the sedimentary formations with which I was familiar. Something was different.

As part of my career with the US Forest Service, I lived and worked four years on or next to Boulder Mountain, west of Capitol Reef National Park in southern Utah. This magnificent lump of sedimentary rocks—capped and protected by lava hardened into basalt—was called the throne of the Colorado Plateau, bumping the clouds at 11,000 feet, with its nearly flat top a paradise of meadows and lakes intermingled with spruce forests.

As I worked and explored the lower stretches of the mountain, stretching into Capitol Reef National Park and the Waterpocket Fold, I became very familiar with such formations as Navajo, Wingate, Moenkopi, Kayenta. I thought I understood the long geologic history of this wonderland of cliffs and canyons carved into the red and white sandstones and mudstones that told a fantastic story of Earth's history.

After leaving Utah for several years, I retired from the Forest Service but returned to western Colorado as the call of the Colorado Plateau pulled me like a magnet back to the edge of the slickrock country. Now, with plenty of free time, I studied the interesting new geologic attractions—the Black Canyon of the Gunnison, Grand Mesa, the San Juan Mountains—and how they fit into the overall picture of all those sedimentary rocks and canyons.

After I became Artist-in-Residence of the NCA in 2017, with the purpose of writing a book of essays about the area, I needed to understand this canyon country better, but that required more study of its geology. After wading through geologic texts and talking to geologists, one day my wife asked if I knew more about the area now. I said, "No, I know even less." That is the enigma of this canyon country. The more you study, the more confused you get. And this particular area—which is at the intersection of the main Colorado Rockies uplift, the Black Canyon uplift, the north-trending downslope of the Piceance Basin, the lava-capped Grand Mesa, the volcanic West Elk Mountains and adjacent San Juan Mountains, and the ancient uplift of the Uncompahgre Plateau—all combined to add confusion to scenic beauty.

I was unable to just accept the scenic beauty without wondering how it came to be. I've always felt that people should understand the very earth at their feet. In this part of the world, that earth extends into a visible past well over one billion years as evidenced by the very rock at my feet. My home and property east of the NCA is now a boulder-strewn mesa, once part of Grand Mesa before a monstrous landslide that occurred over 600,000 years ago. But it was also once underneath a huge Cretaceous sea and covered with thousands of feet of mud. Before that, it was part of seashore and river estuary sands, then Sahara-size desert sand dunes, then more sands and muds and, well, that is what confused me. It rose and fell, folded, and submerged, near the Equator, then moved northwestward along with the entire continent, then at sea level, then above it, trampled by dinosaurs, then mastodons. Is it any wonder I confused myself?

Once, this area was part of a towering mountain range, which was then eroded into nothing, then covered with sediments, then another mountain range, then back to sea level. "As steady and solid as the very Earth" takes on a new meaning, and a rather empty meaning at that, when you learn more about this very Earth. It is not very solid or permanent. But that emphasizes what I knew as a biologist and ecologist. Change is what is permanent. Nothing stays the same. Don't count on anything being there forever, even the very ball of rock called Earth. And if you want to confuse yourself even further, study quantum physics and cosmology, which goes back to the very beginning of time and the universe.

"Enough," I cried. I wanted to just fade into one of those red rock canyons and stare at the cliffs the rest of my life. I still know less than when I started. Isn't that the basis of the old saying "the more you know, the more you don't know?"

In this collection I have tried to capture some of the history, the geology, the magnetic pull of the canyon country. And as I contemplated the geology, I tried to think about how I and my kind fit in the big picture. If I leave you a little confused or bewildered, then join the club. Maybe we shouldn't know everything there is to know. Some degree of mystery can be character building.

J.A.C. 1-1-18

What's in a Name?

Rocks and waters...are words of God,
and so are men. We all flow from one fountain.
John Muir

I STOOD ALONG THE river, watching it roll relentlessly yet quietly down the canyon. The river itself is a living entity, carrying unknown secrets of its origin, its life, its power. It was named Gunnison, after a military explorer and surveyor who visited this area over 150 years ago. Besides the river, Gunnison also had a national forest, a county, a town, a multitude of other streets, birds and plants named after him. All this for a man who only came through the area once or twice and got himself killed by Indians over in Utah. What is in a name? What did he do to deserve such a lasting epitaph? He did "discover" the river that he called *Grand,* which was later renamed in his honor. The Ute and their ancestors had known and lived near the river for millennia. The Ute called it by a long name that meant "the river with many rocks and much water."

I was standing near Dominguez and Escalante canyons, named after two explorers who never stood on or even near this spot. They both left legacies of name scattered throughout the West, for simply wandering by, doing very little to enhance anyone's life, although they also "discovered" a region well-known to the people who had lived there for thousands of years.

What gave mapmakers and name-givers the right to start naming things that already had names? Did the ancients—

those people before the Ute and those we call Fremont and Anasazi—name places and things? For most places we don't know and probably never will. But I like to think the people who left the pictographs and petroglyphs, the hearths and stone structures, called this river of life something special. Something like *life giver* or *waters of the man above*. A name that meant something, describing a value or meaning. What arrogance our modern ancestors had in thinking they had discovered something new and placed their own names on everything.

Names. Is it important we know this plant is called a skunkbush sumac or rhus trilobata? Or that bird flying high above is a golden eagle or aquila chrysaetos? It is much more important we know the plant produced berries that made a great drink. Or the eagle may have been revered as a mighty hunter with symbolic feathers, able to transfer power to a new wearer of the feathers.

Gunnison was looking for a railroad route through the Rockies. Did he understand the Ute and their relationship with the land they had lived in for centuries? Did Father Escalante know how the natives relied on the bighorn sheep for food, clothing, and other things? That is why the ancients depicted sheep on so much of their rock art.

We name everything. We call the cliff forming red sandstone by the name Wingate. Do we understand why it is cliff-forming and that it often is the source of seeps and springs that gave life to the people living in this desert country? North of here is a national monument comprised of Wingate sandstone cliffs. These cliffs overlook the town of Grand Junction. Do the people of Grand Junction, who see these cliffs towering west of town every day, realize they were once a huge Sahara-like desert stretching for hundreds of miles south and west? With no land plants or animals to speak of nearly 200 million years ago? Huge oceans, mudflats, and sand deserts took turns covering this country. No one was there to name them. They were just there, passing time and creating rock that millions of years later we would arrogantly name after whatever we felt appropriate.

I reached into the water of that river of life and turned over a rock. Little insect larva squiggled off it. I don't know their names. I bet the Ute understood which ones produced the insects that the native cutthroat trout relied on for spring feasts.

I looked up into the sky and saw the artistic swirl of clouds. They have a name. I could look at a chart and know the type of cloud. The ancients didn't need a weather map or forecast to predict the weather. They would have glanced at the sky and said those were clouds that meant rain. A soft *female rain* that gently fell all day and night, or a *male rain* that meant fierce winds and lightning. They didn't worry about names. They worried about meanings and relationships.

I used to know names, common and scientific. I needed that information for my job. What I would rather have known were the secrets these long-departed ancients took with them. We lost libraries of knowledge when we ignored their wisdom and renamed everything, most of which meant nothing except a legacy for someone totally undeserving.

What is in a name? It depends on what the name means and who bestowed it upon an object or place. The name San Juan Mountains means St. John. It really means nothing other than the name giver was a devout religious person who was honoring a saint of the Christian religion. Uncompahgre is a Ute name that meant something like red water or dirty water, because the water leaving the highlands of the Uncompahgre Plateau and the nearby mineral-rich San Juan Mountains was red or dirty because of eroding soil. A band of the Ute people is named Uncompahgre, a name with meaning for a group of people displaced from the place they lived for millennia.

A name can describe something—its physical characteristic such as color or taste or value for people or animals. It can describe its history or its association with something else. Somewhere along the line we decided a name, instead, should honor a person, whether he or she had anything to do with the object.

I think I will look to the east and call that mass of rock "Thunder Mountain," as the Ute did. It is really not a *mesa* and it may be *grand*, but that name means nothing to me; and I will call this canyon "black rock bottom with red rock sides" rather than Dominguez. Maybe I will have to invent a word that reduces that long name to one or two words, perhaps simply: "magic."

ALONG THE TABEGUACHE

Sit down before fact like a little child,
and be prepared to give up every preconceived notion,
follow humbly to wherever and whatever abyss nature leads
or you shall learn nothing.
T.H. Huxley

TABEGUACHE IS A Ute word meaning "people of sun mountain." This comes from the Uto-Aztecan word *Tava* meaning sun or chief. Or at least in some interpretations. The Ute language gets a little difficult and like many native languages, can be rather intimidating to English speakers. Uncompahgre—a widely used word in this area of Colorado— means red water, so the Uncompahgre band of Utes were people of red water. This reflects the reddish runoff from the acres of red sandstone and iron-rich deposits in volcanic rocks to the south.

The National Conservation Area makes up the northeastern edge of the Uncompahgre Plateau, the high-elevation ridge of land in western Colorado. But it is all one integral part of the landscape and tied together in a web of geology, biology and history.

It is also host to a portion of the Tabeguache Trail that wends from west of Grand Junction southerly to near Montrose for almost 150 miles. Hikers, bicyclers, ATV riders, four-wheelers, and horse riders can use all or parts of this trail that covers a spectrum of rock and grass, trees and cliffs. And open spaces. Lots of open spaces that tell many stories—if people only stop to listen.

Listen to the quiet, the wind, the birds, the breathing of the very earth. The story goes back a few hundred years, when the Tabeguache and Uncompahgre roamed this land, and even further, when their ancestors explored their back yard thousands of years ago. Then even further, when the giant bison and mammoth wandered by, then even further, when the dinosaurs thundered across the plains, then to before anything wandered or flew or even swam.

This land is old. Stand on the divide between Gibbler Gulch and Big Dominguez Canyon and look in all directions. You can see well over one billion years of history as told by the rocks. One billion years and counting. There are over one billion stars in just one galaxy in the night sky, lost in a billion galaxies. Math becomes overwhelming if you let it. You become a meaningless speck if you try and think about all this.

As I looked towards Gibbler Mountain, what impressed me was not what I saw, but what I didn't see. I didn't see layers of millions of years of sands and muds turned to rock. Formations now eroded away, long washed to the shores of an ocean that has increased and widened to something almost as vast as the billions we just thought about. Billions of grains of sand now being formed into new rock under billions of gallons of saltwater.

At the bottom of Big Dominguez Canyon, and underlying everything you can see from up here, is the basement rock of a schist and granitic gneiss, black and grey. That is the original rock that extends down into Mother Earth until the mantle disappears into the magma encircling the core of the Earth. There is nothing more recent underneath it, although we really don't know for sure exactly what is underneath it. But there must be something older. Schist is a metamorphosed sandstone—sands deposited on something else, then transformed by intense heat. We say it is over a billion years old, but the very Earth is four billion. What happened in that first three billion years?

Overlying the basement rock are the formations that cover the Colorado Plateau—Wingate, Morrison, Dakota, Chinle, Mancos. A list that goes on, familiar to anyone who has marveled at the slickrock paradise extending past Moab to the west, south to Arizona and the Grand Canyon, north to Wyoming and beyond. A whole—tied together by the rock and its exposure—sometimes hidden, sometimes gone.

What is gone as I look over Gibbler Gulch? Thousands of feet of sandstone, shale, limestone, and what else? They are no longer there. I wonder if this is what the Moab country—the fantasyland of red cliffs and canyons to our west—will look like in a few million years. It seems rather drab and featureless, but look in the nooks and crannies and you see hints. The canyons of Dominguez and Escalante—the rock underneath the basalt cap of Grand Mesa to the east—are a jigsaw puzzle that I need someone else to assemble for me. This is a peek-a-boo country, hiding a history that has more excitement than any thousand James Bond or Indiana Jones movies.

It is a story of life itself, from when life struggled in an endless ocean, to the thundering terrible lizards, to modern-day mammals, many of whom—such as the native North American horse, mammoth, saber-toothed smilodon and giant ground sloth—no longer wander this Earth.

This land is vast and still mostly unknown, hiding secrets we can never guess. Our time here, even that of the Tabeguache and Uncompahgre and their distant ancestors, is so miniscule, it is a drop of water in that distant ocean. As I stand and gaze at that history, the wind blows endlessly as it has for a billion days and nights. It waves the ricegrass and blue grama in its constant but changing breeze, drawing perfect circles in the sand around the stems. It carries the raven upward in thermals as the wind comes out of the baking hot canyon below, to this cooler height of a ridge.

I can see the distant outlines of Unaweep Canyon to the north, still a mystery of geologic wonder. What force carved this miniature Yosemite? Was it the ancestral Colorado or Gunnison River? Or a glacier falling off the higher uplands of the Uncompahgre Plateau? The Unaweep Canyon walls are the same gneiss and schist (with a hint of granite) underlying the Plateau, once covered by thousands of feet of that same rock that has been worn away, gone too, as surely as the glaciers that surrounded this country as recently as only a few thousand years ago.

I look up as building cumulus clouds herald a July thunderstorm. A storm that will pelt the rock with rain and hail in a never-ending attempt to remove even more rock. Someday there will be a flat, featureless plain which existed here once before, several million years ago. Time repeats itself in cycles and circles. The Tabeguache people probably understood cycles and circles. That was what life was about.

Eventually, at some point in a distant future, maybe even a billion years or so, someone—if there are any beings around to contemplate such things—might stand in this very spot and wonder about the past. There will be no Gibbler Gulch or Gibbler Mountain, no Dominguez Canyon, no Colorado or Gunnison Rivers and certainly no canyons or high plateaus. And no Tabeguache Trail or memory of a people called Tabeguache or Americans. But the wind will still blow and rain will still fall from blackening cumulus clouds on what might be a July afternoon.

BIG DOMINGUEZ

Wilderness is the bank on which all checks are drawn.
John Aspinwall

IT WAS A warm June morning, soon to become a hot June day, typical of this part of Colorado. Not the best time of year to be hiking Big Dominguez, but this was to be our maiden hike into this red rock canyon. I needed to see the mysteries of this wilderness all times of year. Life in this canyon continues day-to-day as it adjusts to seasons and climate. Human comfort is not a measure of meaning.

Hiking along the river was peaceful as the green water flowed calmly between the red rock walls, accompanied by a wide trail and a railroad track. Wilderness draped the west side of the river, with its hidden secrets, but civilization still fought to hold onto the east side. A highway, traffic, people, and towns lurked behind the east canyon wall. My attention was west.

Meeting Becca—the BLM wilderness ranger—was enjoyable as she gave us information and a welcome to her domain. It brought back memories of my greeting visitors to the terrains of my past, similar to Becca, but in different times and places. A friendly greeting by the local expert always means a lot, particularly if that official cares and wants to share. I could tell Becca assumed a pride of ownership in this, her territory.

After walking past the rickety and historic old bridge, now closed to all but the occupant of the ranch across the river, we crossed the green water below on a new public hiking bridge. Turning south, the trail continued alongside the river. Walking beneath the Wingate cliffs reinforced old memories; it was like coming home to an old friend. However, here, the cliffs were more broken, with large chunks of rock breaking up the usual Wingate smooth, slick walls. A Bullock's oriole, chattering from the riverbank tangle of tall grass and tamarisk, had already welcomed us.

Cottonwoods lined the trail a few yards away from the river itself, sprouted years ago and once watered by a long-abandoned irrigation ditch paralleling the trail. The ditch did not now give enough water to keep the trees vigorous; massive dead limbs indicated evidence of better days. New cottonwoods along the river were protected by fencing. Beavers, I supposed, held sway along the river, anxious to nibble any new growth in an otherwise treeless river bank. Hopefully, efforts to rid the river of the invasive tamarisk would eventually allow for more of the native cottonwood to reappear after years of absence. Closer to the river, they would not be dependent on the long-abandoned ditch.

There were a few other signs that someone once tried to use this area for something that required a fence or water flume, but that time was long gone. Leaving the river, the trail passed a sign that declared we were entering official wilderness. The canyon walls looked the same to me, but that aura hung over the canyon—we were now in an area where we were visitors who did not remain. I had no intention of remaining, but at one time, people did. This was their home and they knew nothing about a concept called wilderness. To the ancients, there was no such thing as wilderness. All of it was home.

I soon noticed we were walking on the bedrock that formed the floor of the canyon. It was purplish-black, but covered with broken deposits of white quartz. We soon left the confluence of Big and Little Dominguez, about the time I first heard the haunting call of the canyon wren, my favorite bird and symbol of slickrock cliffs and canyons.

I kept my eyes peeled for quartz crystals in the white patches of rock. I didn't find any, but I was intrigued by the combination of red sandstone walls framing a wide canyon floor made up of the dark gneiss or schist, interspersed with fractured white quartz deposits.

The prickly pear cactus had bloomed weeks before, during a low-country springtime, now a distant memory. The heat of summer, bouncing off the red rock walls, would soon make this an unpleasant hike. But it was still morning, so we could make a mile or more before calling retreat.

I scanned the cliffs for bighorn sheep and listened for the canyon wren. I saw neither but did hear the occasional call of the cliff-dwelling small bird. Seeing and hearing these small feathered residents always brings a smile to me. They act as my companions, listening with feigned interest as I try to imitate their calls. They are naturally inquisitive and keep me company as I visit their domain. They are not possessive as my species tends to be, but seem to be saying "come and visit and I will entertain you. I will be your friend."

I knew the falls of Big Dominguez Creek were not far ahead and these were touted as one of the main attractions of this long canyon. When we first came along the creek, there were a series of small cascades, which I wondered if they were the falls. If so, I was a little disappointed. They weren't, and I wasn't. A little further, the trail came alongside a bedrock outcrop with a jumble of stream channels digging into the hard rock, leaving smooth water-worn passages. Wandering onto this water maze, I discovered the falls. They were sideways. The creek comes onto this outcrop and instead of continuing straight, takes a ninety-degree turn and dives off the edge. A couple dozen feet below, it then continues on its eastward course, a small trickle in such a large canyon.

The layout of this jumble of hard rock intrigued me. It was not typical of a straight line waterfall in a normal creek. What happened here that blocked the stream and caused it to take a quick ninety-degree turn and fall, then continue along as if nothing had happened? There was no hard rock companion on the south side of the creek. It was a continuation of the talus and dirt slope angling up to the south canyon wall. The explanation had to be a fault or some geologic anomaly that I needed a geologist to explain, but there was no one handy. I tried not to worry about the whys and let myself enjoy the pure water tumbling over the edge of a twenty-foot fall. I almost succeeded.

It was time to turn back as the noontime heat was starting to sap my energy, but I sat for a while, imagining what was in this big canyon for the next dozen miles. That would have to wait. I knew it would not be more of the same, as each turn in the trail offered different views and perspectives. And I knew there was rock art hidden on the red walls. Sometimes, leaving surprises for the future is the enticing motivation for further exploration. I know from experience the call of unexplored places. This will be one; the tantalizing first couple miles left me wanting more. I will visit the Big D again, but sometimes we all need to keep a special place for a future that often never comes. Whether it does or doesn't, knowing it is there is all I need.

ESCALANTE CANYON

Learn from yesterday, live for today,
hope for tomorrow. The important thing
is not to stop questioning.
Albert Einstein

ESCALANTE CANYON IS the area of the NCA familiar to most people. It is where civilization tried to tame this canyon country. The main Gunnison River corridor has been lined by a railroad track, but no through roads. A few orchards and ranches dot the main river and the main Escalante Canyon. But development in this magnificent canyon is mostly visible nowadays by signs of former habitation, not by current lives save a few hardy souls.

Determined pioneers tried to settle the canyon, and did for a while. The recent human history is an interesting read in itself, captured in great detail by Muriel Marshall's *Red Hole in Time* (Texas A&M University Press, 1988). The history, like much post-Ute history of this area of western Colorado, is an interesting episode in the struggle of optimistic pioneers to inhabit a difficult piece of country, trying to put it to uses not designed by nature.

The early human residents thousands of years ago had no trouble fitting in. They brought only themselves and a history of adapting. I can only guess about this conclusion since I wasn't there and I never lived that type of life. As to the more recent settlers, I can guess that trying to adapt an Illinois or Missouri lifestyle, farming or ranching with animals not adapted to this harsh climate and terrain, would have been very difficult. The end result is what we see in Escalante Canyon—evidence of past lives, but only a few current lives.

Captain Smith's cabin and the Walker cabin, both currently part of the Colorado State Wildlife Area system, are well-visited historic sites. Names, such as Musser, Ben Lowe, and Huffington, along with many others, haunt this canyon like spirits looking for peace after years of struggle. Pioneers who found a paradise walled in by red rock cliffs may have found life too difficult and too isolated in this canyon. Maybe they brought too much with them. Excess baggage did not fit. The Ute and earlier residents may have had a tough learning curve as well, but they carried little baggage that burdened them. They left signs of their lives as well, but pictographs and petroglyphs require very little maintenance. Stand in the right place and you can see the petroglyphs but you can also hear the names of the pioneer settlers bounce off the cliffs like echoes fading in time.

The canyon was settled before access was developed. There was no bridge across the Gunnison River, although the railroad was an early presence. The settlers came to and from Delta and civilization via Sawmill Mesa and a tricky path down into Dry Creek and across Escalante Creek. This lack of easy access made living in the canyon a test of survival. Today you can drive the well-maintained county road across the Gunnison Bridge and up the canyon, pausing to feel the loneliness that once fought with civilization. I think loneliness won the battle.

Cross Escalante Creek when the water is low and drive up Dry Fork Canyon on a hair-raising steep and rocky road and onto Dry Mesa. The miles stretch by, underlining that feeling of loneliness. Further up onto the Uncompahgre Plateau, which never really ends or begins, you can enter the national forest and come into dinosaur country. The Dry

Bench Quarry, hidden in the pines, has given up a world-class supply of dinosaur bones and tracks, including new species never seen before. Almost 2500 feet in elevation below this quarry, the trickle of water called Escalante Creek that enters the Gunnison River belies the fact that this same creek, over time, has probably excavated more earth and rock than humankind has excavated in its entire history. And it still continues, grain by grain and pebble by pebble. The line of descendants of the early Escalante Canyon settlers probably also continues, great-grandchild by great-great-grandchild, but far removed from the canyon and their ancestors. How many descendants are there from over ten thousand years of the ancients who also lived here?

Escalante Canyon, along with neighbors Big and Little Dominguez to the north, and Cottonwood to the south, are just four of many canyons and drainages that carve in almost straight lines into the east slope of the Uncompahgre Plateau. Not only is this an old landscape, it is massive. But it is different from the glacially-carved canyons and high snow-capped peaks of the main Rockies or San Juans to the east and south. It is dry and starkly majestic in comparison. Sometimes the overlooked hides serendipitous discoveries. Escalante Canyon is the showpiece of the NCA in terms of easy accessibility. It is a massive canyon, much wider than the elusive and secretive Big and Little Dominguez just a few tortuous miles beyond the northern rim of the canyon wall.

The main road doesn't stop at Escalante Forks, but most drivers do. A very difficult road leads south and up out of the canyon. An easier road leads north and west onto Bennetts Basin and then miles across the uplands of the Uncompahgre. But the canyon keeps going west after roads stop. Actually several canyons keep going since there is a reason for the name Escalante Forks. Several canyons converge (or split) at this point and continue west. If you can get to an overlook somewhere up on the canyon rim at this point, you can see the trademark red Wingate cliffs continue, slowly sinking into the rising uplift. They eventually disappear, yet-to-be uncovered by time and erosion. They are a work in progress, leaving the comforts of civilization far behind.

To get the true feel of this canyon, you must come back more than once, in more than one season. It is a serendipity of hidden secrets, a preview of the canyon country to the west, over the big Uncompahgre Plateau and into the vast expanse of the Colorado Plateau in Utah. On second thought, maybe secrets are best kept secret.

BENNETTS BASIN

Although the myriad things are many, their order is one.
Chuang Tzu

THE HIGH PLATEAU between Escalante Canyon and Little Dominguez on the west end of the NCA is called Bennetts Basin. It is also the head of Camp Ridge, Sowbelly Ridge, Tatum Ridge, Palmer Gulch, Bad Point and Good Point. A place with many names, it is a plateau that defies time. It is what remains after all the adjacent canyons eroded away. It is what the country used to look like before gravity and water did their artistry. Lacking the dramatic views and exposure of the surrounding canyons, this area offers a relaxing contrast, as if letting you catch your breath.

The historic McCarty Trail and old Gunnison Stock Trail pass through on their way from the river bottom to the high Uncompahgre to the west. There is very little bedrock exposed, although the pinyon-juniper landscape is dotted with broken sandstone rocks and small boulders. It is easy to reach Bennetts from Escalante Forks, but not easy to circle around to anywhere else, at least by road: you must go back down the way you came up from the Forks, or traverse the high Uncompahgre Plateau for miles.

I have talked before about the immensity of this country. Standing on the rim of either Escalante or Big Dominguez Canyons, the NCA seems to go on forever. When you can see the expanse of the Uncompahgre Plateau to the west, you gain a new understanding of the word *awe*. The totality of the Uncompahgre Plateau, including national forest and

BLM, is larger than Rhode Island or Delaware. Canyons and valleys radiate to the east and west, aligned in long fingers of ridge and canyon. This is not a dendritic pattern common to the rest of the Colorado Rockies.

As I drove west from Bennetts Basin, I could not stop gawking at the openness and the span of land that seems to go on forever. I have stood on Engineer Pass in the nearby San Juan Mountains and marveled at the magnificent peaks and valleys. The openness of the Uncompahgre Plateau west of Dominguez-Escalante NCA is different. The canyons of the NCA are the bottom, the opening up of the massif of the Plateau. They are the end product of what erosion will eventually do to the higher country to the south, north, and west.

That thought struck me as I tried to look down the upper ends of the canyons, now broad valleys. The high country has more Dominguez and Escalante Canyons hidden under the verdant surface. The high country receives water, in the form of rain and snow, that the lower country does not. The aspen, fir and spruce, mingled with oakbrush and grasslands, were replaced by rock cliffs and cactus, mingled with juniper and pinyon lower down in the NCA. Those canyons were once buried far beneath the surface, probably covered with spruce and fir. We can only guess. I don't know how high the ancestral Uncompahgre Mountains were. Their underlying mass was the sedimentary layers now shorn from their surface as well as the surface of the lower canyon igneous rocks.

In my thinking, to know and understand the geology of this part of the West is to know and understand the mind of God. Even though I know the basics of sedimentation and rising and uplifting, it still addles my mind to comprehend it. Rising and retreating seas and broad coastlines were covered with sands, the limestones, the muds. Flat river mouths miles long, of continental rivers possibly came all the way from the eroding Appalachians far to the east. The north-south axis of the Uncompahgre Plateau is a rising lump on the land, whose east side dives under the Mancos Shale bottom of the broad valley to the east. Right about where the lava-capped Grand Mesa covers a north-south trending basin that sinks under the northwest corner of Colorado. South of that, the dome of the uplifted Black Canyon brought sub-surface black rocks to the surface, quickly eroding the softer sedimentary rocks that now sit under Grand Mesa. Understanding this "Geology 101 course" leaves one uncomfortably confident to then understand the San Juan volcanic field, the spine of the Colorado Rockies to the east, and then the broad canyon country of Utah to the west. I never knew how easy I had it where I grew up in flat-as-a-pancake central Illinois, underlain by a simple limestone rock and covered with the richest and blackest soil in the world.

I occasionally dream of being able to simply stand on one of these canyon rims and marvel about the color, the texture, the openness of the straight-as-an-arrow canyons. To be able to exclaim how rugged and how beautiful they are, without trying to understand their origin and history and not worry about where the muds of the Mancos Shale came from. To stand at the foot of the Devils Thumb north of Delta and marvel at the desolateness and sterility of the 'dobie badlands. Never mind that some long-missing mountain range supplied the erosional deposition in that long-gone Cretaceous seaway. Where were those mountains and what were they made of? Were those mountains something close by that long since erased any trace or their location— sandstone of another long-eroded mountain range three geologic generations back in far distant history? Or were they also from the far away Himalayan-high Appalachians? How far back do we go? Remember, the dinosaurs lived less than 200 million years ago on the face of an Earth that was already nearly 4 billion years old.

They say knowledge can be a dangerous thing. Too little knowledge can be even more dangerous. I think back to our ancestors who drew pictures of hands and sheep and snakes on rock walls and lived off the rabbits and sheep that wandered the ancient canyons they called home. Life may have been dangerous and short-lived, but their worries were not about scientific knowledge, rather simply staying alive.

Exploring as much of the Bennetts Basin plateau as I could on primitive dirt roads, I decided I had seen enough. Evidence of recent hunter camps, old cattle corrals and fences were evident, but they defined the common in this country. I was getting used to the more scenic and colorful canyon walls and depths that fell off on each side of this plateau. This in itself was a little dangerous since when we get used to the spectacular, we ignore the not-so-spectacular. As I stood in one of the open areas, seeing hints of the vast landscape below and to the east, I forced myself to appreciate this small expanse of trees and flatness. It is part of my drifting philosophy. We need the fast and dangerous, the whitewater, the broken canyon walls. But we also need the slow and contemplative, the slack water, the mesa tops of flat and monotonous. The yin and the yang. The deer replaces the bighorn, the chickadee replaces the canyon wren. Above it all soars the eagle and the raven. It is all part of the whole and the whole is what makes us. Thank goodness for the Bennetts Basins that allow us to catch our breath. Breathe deeply during these interludes. Then go ride the white water.

THE LOST MANCOS SHALE

One does not discover new lands without consenting
to lose sight of the shore for a very long time.
Andre Gide

THE ATTRACTIONS OF the NCA are the cliffs, mesas, and canyons. What you see is what you get. I know the canyons are the result of erosion, a long geologic process that grinds up rock and spits it out far away in a distant sea. On a day when I was able to see to the east to the nearby mass of Grand Mesa that towered above the horizon, I was struck by the badlands of Mancos Shale at the base of the Mesa. Desolate mudflats and eroded hills, this rock, if you can call it that, was once the bottom of a huge sea bisecting the growing continent of North America. It once spanned several states and lay hundreds and even thousands of feet thick. It also once covered the Uncompahgre Plateau as well as the Black Canyon uplift a few miles upriver.

It is now totally gone west of the Gunnison River. At least until a hundred or so miles west, where it surfaces again to cover hundreds of thousands of acres near Hanksville, Utah. Once again overwhelmed by the vastness of time and rock, I marveled at the thought that all that mud-rock had been removed from the Uncompahgre Plateau, as well as the rock that once covered it. Such as evidenced by the mass of Grand Mesa, until that mass was protected from erosion by the basalt cap that was once a valley floor.

Gone. Forever disappeared. That is the underlying theme of all this land—the whole scene. As magnificent as the canyons and river of the NCA are, they must be seen as part of the larger picture. They represent a small slice of time and place. Within their purview, you see not only the sedimentary layers of time on the vast Colorado Plateau, you see the high peaks of the edge of the Colorado Rockies. The Rockies—seen here as the Ruby Range, Raggeds, West Elks, San Juans, Grand Mesa, and all that lies to the east, culminating in the Continental Divide—all offer different origins and different times in the march of the formation of the Earth.

There is something going on just to the east of the Gunnison River, starting near the location of Highway 50. From there north, south, and east, the Mancos Shale badlands cover the landscape. But not west of the highway and river. Just at this point, the Uncompahgre uplift starts bubbling up the Earth, and the Mancos is nowhere to be seen. No melting muds, no badlands, nothing. What happened here? The huge Cretaceous Seaway that covered what is now several states did cover what is now the Uncompahgre and the thousands of feet of sandstones that still cover much of the Colorado Plateau. After the sea dried up, the plateau started rising once again. The soft Mancos shale was quick to erode away as the mountain chain rose. But the shale just to the east stayed there as the land east of the plateau started going the opposite direction, dipping down into the Piceance Basin.

Each of these areas—the Uncompahgre Plateau, the Piceance Basin, Grand Mesa, the Black Canyon uplift—all have their own stories to tell. They occurred in different times and have different outcomes. Right here, where I try to understand a little of it, they all come together in a confusing tangle of history.

What I find most interesting is that in the far distant future, the river valleys of the Gunnison, Uncompahgre and Colorado will have eroded away the Mancos Shale.

The many layers of sandstone below may then create more canyons like Dominguez right down there where Delta sits in the year 2017. Now that is a thought to contemplate as I turn my attention back to the NCA of the present day. It will not change in my lifetime, but change it will. I only wish I could see the results.

SPRINGTIME AT THE POTHOLES

A creature without memory cannot discover the past.
One without expectation cannot conceive a future.
George Santayana

THE WINDS WERE starting to flow down from the higher plateau as an approaching spring weather system was heading into Colorado from the Great Basin. The warmth of the sunny afternoon started to heat the surrounding canyon walls. Spring green was painting the cottonwoods along the canyon floor while hidden flowers were opening in the seeps along the Wingate cliffs above.

Breathing in this change of seasons, we stood on the inner canyon rim watching the brown flow of spring runoff carry the muddied snowmelt off the Uncompahgre Plateau. Springtime in the Rockies means different things, but on this April day, it meant the stair-step greenup from the lowland canyons of the Escalante slowly upwards to the Plateau far above us. Spring lasts for months in this plateau country.

But my attention at the moment was on the Potholes. This section of Escalante Creek is famous for its dangerous but fascinating drop through the granitic inner canyon of the much larger and mostly sandstone Escalante Canyon. The roar of falling water below us was muffled this day by the rush of the spring winds over pinyon and bare rock above us.

The gray-black of the granitic rock was what drew me, however. Driving up the canyon from the Gunnison River bridge, we were mesmerized by the sandstone cliffs and the tumbled rock of the slowly widening canyon walls. This eastern edge of the vast Colorado Plateau is built from the familiar formations of this part of the West. Entrada, Morrison, Dakota, Wingate, Chinle, and other names that continue to fascinate me are like old friends. But as the road slowly climbed up the canyon floor, the underlying rock climbed as well. All of a sudden the rock turned black—we had arrived at Earth's basement rocks. A totally different kind of rock, indicating no more ancient deserts, seas, and river beds. All that stopped here. From here to the center of the Earth lies the primeval Earth itself. All else above it is icing on the cake. This is the core, the beginning. Nothing significantly different was under our feet until magma. This was an ancient mountain range composed of the granite and gneiss now visible once again along the canyon floor—the ancestral Rockies—that uplifted on this very spot untold ages ago. Then it was eroded away, to be covered by the familiar sedimentary rocks that were uplifted as the area rose once again and are now slowly being eroded and washed to a distant sea.

The basement rock is hard, incredibly hard, so that the running snowmelt of a stream has struggled for millennia to carve out this narrow slit that now claims fame as the Potholes. As the water rushes through the narrow walls and over falls, it swirls and undercuts the very cliff it is falling over. Smooth rock walls without good handholds, the undercutting behind the falls, and the deep eddies, all create an unseen danger to unwary swimmers. Swimmers diving into the seemingly calm pools of water are caught in the swirling undertow and held there. For years, partying young people drowned with disturbing regularity every spring. Land managers and law enforcement stepped in, and with a well-developed parking and picnic area, with signs, and with vigilance, the drownings have decreased as has the partying.

That was the result of management of people. But there is no management of the rock walls. The upper canyon walls still hold people's attention by displaying the red and white of crumbling rock. The canyon wren warbles his descending melody that echoes off the red and black-stained walls. The ravens and eagles soar high above. The lizards and mice scurry in and under the rocks that lie like scattered toys. The fossilized bones of dinosaurs lay hidden deep in the rock that once lay on the surface of this desert. As nearby mountains slowly eroded, the red grains of sand meandered through deltas of mile-wide riverbeds. No rushing spring melt there. The scenery was different then, the plants nothing we see today. All life and all evidence of its presence was slowly covered and hidden, to appear millions of years later as canyon walls we see today.

And beneath it all lies the black-gray granite and gneiss that form a solid foundation. A basement sturdy enough to hold the thousands of feet of sandstone and fossils and secrets hidden for well over 200 million years and counting.

Can people standing here understand this? Do they comprehend what happens in 200 million years? Do they realize the absence of hundreds of millions of years between the black granite and the next layer of red sandstone? In the contact between the black and the red lies the hundreds of millions of missing years between the life that contained only one-celled bacteria and the thundering feet of dinosaurs.

As the canyon streams cut down through the layers of red rock, life slowly evolved in the different layers of time. But when the streams hit the black of the granite, any signs of past life nearly disappeared. Oceans and lava beds that covered the earth at this point knew very little of what we call life.

That is what intrigued me as I listened to the call of the

canyon wren and the muffled roar of the creek below me as it wound through the inner canyon, struggling to pick away grain-by-grain the stubborn rock.

I know the water is coming from snowmelt high up on the forested Plateau. It is a different world up there, with abundant water, flower-filled meadows, streams and lakes, and life. Down here in the desert of red rock, life struggles and adapts, fed begrudgingly by seeps and springs and the seasonal flow of the creek. That is the history of this area, through millions of years. So we spend one hour of a sunny spring day standing here watching the water surge below us. We munch on sandwiches and cookies, thinking of our fleeting life in this outdoor cathedral. *Now* is what we are concerned with, and how we make the best of it. But all around us is life and it is time in motion. What will someone 100 million years from now be able to see and contemplate? Will they think of a spring day long turned to dust when meltwater rushed through a canyon? Will there even be a canyon? Will this all be level plain?

Nothing has stayed the same in this one spot. Life changes, the surface of the Earth changes. Cycles and circles, as the ancients felt as they once stood here like we did today. But they changed as well. As we will. And as the canyon will.

FROG PONDS

Four ducks on a pond, A grass bank beyond.
A blue sky of spring, White clouds on the wing.
What a little thing, To remember for years—
To remember with tears!
William Allingham

THANKFULLY THE SKY was clouding over as we started our hike back up out of the canyon. We had begun at the Upper Dominguez Campground and hiked a couple miles down-canyon, July temperatures threatening to continue a sizzling heat wave. Increasing clouds did not produce any rain but did keep the heat down a little, as if 90 degrees feels much more comfortable than 95.

Becca, my BLM wilderness-ranger hiking companion, was now in her comfort space. This was Wilderness, with a capital W. We were reminded we were visitors in nature's comfort space. The map indicated the trail was not maintained, although it was well trod and obvious. A few low-hanging branches did occasionally get in the way, but offered a welcome challenge. I have always found trails to be a way of getting from somewhere to somewhere else—a means to an end. But I was slowly changing my perspective: a trail could be the ends, not the means. I found my original objective of getting far down the canyon to be intimidating: a long way down the canyon just so I could see what was down there. I had a good idea what I would see was similar to what I was seeing where I was, probably a pine- and juniper-dotted canyon with red rock walls and a small stream wandering down the middle. I know the view and all the little details vary step-by-step on a long trail like this, but this was not the day for me to find out. Isn't that what I had heard people say for years about similar trails. "It's all the same: forest or high tundra or desert." I never held this attitude since every new turn in the trail offered new rewards.

But I knew I would come back later and wander aimlessly in search and exploration. Along the north canyon wall, I would touch the Wingate sandstone cliffs that border the canyon. There were lots of tumble-down rocks and boulders, all of which offered treasures of shape and texture. Nooks and crannies in the cliff wall often hold secrets. The fallen boulders, some large as a house, were to me unusual for Wingate, whose red sandstone cliffs are notorious for very little rockfall. Erosion is normally smooth, with not much talus or large boulders at cliff bottoms.

And yet, on this day I began to see my experience and my surroundings with fresh eyes. I found the pinyon forest intriguing: open and scattered amongst smallish juniper, with little undergrowth. Even though the trail wound through this forest, I found my aimless wandering between the trees and rocks was rewarding. Gnarled, twisted tree trunks dotted the ground like works of art standing in a museum. They were truly nature's sculptures.

Wandering to the south found me quickly reaching the small stream, nearly hidden in the tangle of willow, alder, rush, horsetail and cattails. I had not seen alder in this area previously, although it is not uncommon in higher elevations near water. The horsetail reached nearly five feet tall pushing up through the alders, as did patches of rush. The riparian area was narrow, since the stream was incised deeply into the black rock, rising steeply on either side. The small stream continued its run down from the higher Plateau to the west. This same water would eventually cascade over the falls miles below before entering into the anonymity of the powerful Gunnison.

I didn't dare wander off-trail near the trailhead since this was the area of what the BLM folks call the *frog ponds*: a flat and broad valley bottom covered with a wetland ecosystem. The falls further down the canyon prevent any fishery up here, but the habitat is ripe for frogs, dragonflies and beaver. I marveled at the few old beaver ponds, especially in an area lacking larger trees. One old cottonwood lay in a pile of shoreline pinyon, with its beaver-gnawed trunk hanging twenty feet in the air. I had to laugh at the surprise of that beaver when he finished felling the tree, which may have thrown him twenty feet into the air as it tumbled over and hung up on the hillside.

This area at the upper end of Dominguez Canyon made me think of what this could have looked like millions of years ago. Instead of normal-sized dragonflies, I might have seen dragonflies the size of golden eagles. Instead of beaver, I might have seen or heard the stegosaurus or even ultrasaurus. This riparian meadow full of cattails and rushes, water and lily pads seemed out of place, although a few miles upstream, I could wander through high elevation meadows and grasslands at an elevation of almost 10,000 feet. This long and interesting Wilderness canyon with the rock-walled sides continues east fourteen miles until it empties into the Gunnison River and the edge-end of a geologically strange uplift called Uncompahgre.

THE STORM: CANYON LIFE

What color is lightning? Where does
the thunder go when it dies?
Ray Bradbury

DEEP IN THE canyon, I was surrounded by red rocks, white rocks, and brown rocks, mingled with red-orange soil dotted with cactus, single leaf ash, scraggly juniper and other assorted plants that somehow thrive in this harsh setting. And above it all a blue sky being invaded with streamers of white clouds. The air had been as still as the lizard watching me from a red rock. Now a few wafts of breeze kicked up. I knew something was coming. The air had the tension of anticipation.

I wandered uphill to the base of the Wingate cliff. A small seep came from a large crack in the sandstone wall. Green ferns, red monkeyflowers, yellow columbines and white watercress created a rich miniature flower garden. Focusing on the variety of life in this small oasis, I failed to notice the sky as it lost its brilliant blue to a growing cover of clouds. Initially white, the clouds thickened and turned a light grey, then darker grey, then lumpy dark blue. The wind had picked up and was swirling red dust in curtains rising, then falling. I could hear a deep rumbling far off to the west, out of sight, hidden by the towering canyon walls. I was in a narrow slot that hid most of the outside world.

That rumbling world was encroaching, however, as I huddled close under the overhang that hid even more of the darkening sky. Thunder was booming closer and louder. Even the birds stopped twittering. A flash of brilliant electric white light was followed within two seconds by an ear-splitting crash, which then echoed throughout the canyon. Far above, lightning went from cloud-to-cloud, branching, forking, flashing. Thunder was sharp and brief, but also echoed low and rumbling, filling the sky like a base drummer's improvisation; close by, it was frightening, far away it was more rhythmic. Either way, the thunder echoed as it bounced from canyon wall to canyon wall, then over the mesa and into adjacent canyons. It echoed until the energy of its atoms and nuclear forces was finally expended.

In the meantime, a few drops of rain hit the rocks. They seemed hesitant to increase, but danced around as if testing the air. As the wind increased, the rain increased. It became a steady, hard rain, but I felt that the deluge was yet to come. I was right. As the lightning and thunder increased, the rain opened up. It fell as if poured from buckets—vertical, horizontal, stinging in its fierce intensity. It bounced off the rocks, swirling as it searched for the place it wanted to settle. Slowly, but with determination, water started flowing down the rounded rocks, then the canyon wall itself. A few small rivulets turned into small waterfalls, then small streams that cascaded, fell, caressed the sandstone. The whole canyon was flowing. The stream below roared as red-brown mud joined the current. The noise was deafening as the running water added harmony to the still echoing thunder. And the day had long ago turned to night.

I was caught in an eerie hypnotic state as the rain, wind, and lightning combined into a fury that held me, afraid to move, afraid to look around. Even though I knew I was safe, nestled in a small alcove in the cliff wall, I was still terrified by the fury unleashed by this passing storm. One lightning flash was simultaneous with the thunder, a loud clap that shook my teeth. I hoped the thunderous vibrations would not loosen any rock on the cliff wall above me.

The lightning was now further east and the rain was letting up, almost turning to hail. I knew that the arrival of hail usually meant the dying fury of a thunderstorm. It was this time as well. The rain turned to a light shower, then stopped as suddenly as it began. The sky lightened, then bright blue appeared in breaks in the dark clouds. The sound that filled my senses was that of running water. Small streams and cascades that still fell down the cliffs searched out the stream that had grown tenfold.

As the bright blue sky rolled the remaining clouds eastward to harass the Grand Mesa and the mountain wall of the far horizon, the birds started singing and the ravens took to the sky to sample the freshness of the ozone-cleansed air. The flow of water slowly eased off the rock walls, but still echoed as a roar as the main canyon now collected the miles of small rivulets into a rushing river. I could hear small boulders crash as they rolled down the torrent, slowly chipping off sharp edges to gain the polished and rounded form that signaled a journey in such floods as this. Time and water working to soften edges, on rock as it does on people.

Still mesmerized by the drama I had witnessed, I sat on a rock now drying in the bright sunlight. Such brief storms as this have painted the July sky for eons. This is the desert and this is what creates and nourishes the persistent life that flourishes here. Life doesn't come easy, nor do the rains and snows. In a few hours, the sand will dry, the low spots turn from pond to wet mud to cracked mud. Rocks have been shifted, streambeds altered, new gullies formed. An ancient scraper or potsherd may have been unearthed somewhere in this canyon, seeing sunlight for the first time in ten thousand years. In places, the stream-bed may be a millimeter deeper.

The canyon is slow to deepen and widen by storms

like this, millimeter by millimeter. I enjoy the warmth of the sun, now melting the few pockets of hail still left in the shade of the rock wall. The clouds, now fading beyond the Continental Divide miles away, are silent, although I know they still carry the fury of sound and wind in the high country. I leave the thought to that other world, so different from where I sit. For now, I breathe in the freshness of enriched life. Canyon life.

SOLAR ECLIPSE

The fairest thing we can experience is the mysterious.
It is the fundamental emotion which stands
at the cradle of true art and science.
Albert Einstein

LATE MORNING ON Monday, August 21, 2017, was like any other summer morning along the Gunnison River. The new moon was nearly invisible in the bright summer sky. The sun was making its usual rounds across the blue vastness from east to west. The ravens and magpies flew over the green fields of Escalante Canyon making their usual noisome racket, and the river still flowed green and fast, although flow was down from an earlier summer high. Snow in the high country was mostly gone and summer rains had eased off in the recent hot and dry spell.

The sky began turning yellow-orange, and light was fading, as if the skies were blotted out by nearby wildfire smoke. It was not smoke though. The eclipse had started. Widely hyped and heralded as a celebrity event, the eclipse was the center of attention nationwide: the sun and moon intersecting for a brief while during their journeys through space. This has happened thousands, if not millions, of times since the sun, moon, and Earth have co-existed.

The river has reflected the shadow of the moon for as long as it has flowed past these red cliffs. The sandstone of the canyon walls has seen the sun disappear, casting midnight darkness over the valley floor. This is nothing new for this land. It was new for those of us standing in the shadows of the red cliffs near the rolling river on this particular day.

We get excited over normal events which occur in our time. The time of the events is measured in millennia and not months or years as is our time. Thus the eclipse was a significant event for us. In this location at this time, we lost nearly 90% of the sun. It was—for those who could see it through darkened glasses or pinholes in pieces of paper—a crescent shape, a thin sliver nearly eaten by our nearby moon. Miles to the northeast, our neighbors witnessed complete darkness for a few minutes. Animals in that path of totality reacted as we would expect. Daytime had turned to night time. Not so here on the Gunnison.

Daylight faded but life continued as it had for millions of years. The sun that cast shadows on the sand dunes of what is now the Wingate sandstone, the moon that lit up a star-filled sky over the adjacent sea, are the same ones we see today. However, the skies are different, the moon is further away, the sun is at a slightly different angle and position. The continents have moved, the landscape not at all like we see today. But the moon still crosses in front of the sun during the day and the Earth shadow still crosses the moon during the night.

Eclipses are not new, nor are shooting stars. The Milky Way is still there, but constellations have changed. Orion was not always there, nor was the Big Dipper. What we think constant, is not over time.

So those of us who watched the eclipse and were in awe of its power and effect on us can be part of the unfolding drama of our Earth and our sun and our moon. It will happen again and again, but what the eclipse casts a shadow on will change. Who will watch it a million years from now?

We get excited about the shadows of an eclipsed sun. What about the shadows of a full-moon-sky? Not as rare as the eclipse shadows, the monthly shadows of a full moon are to me just as special. This is when the night comes alive in a ghostly apparition. Light enough to walk by, but still dark enough to cast the view as an uncertain world.

What about other cosmological phenomena? We see meteors streaking to Earth from the heavens almost daily. Have some fallen here in these canyons? Most likely. Did the native people see them and think the sky was falling? Almost certainly there are a few rocks scattered among the billions lying around in these canyons and on the mesas that came from Mars or the moon or from the asteroid belt where untold billions more are circling the sun. And what happened on that day 65 million years ago when the asteroid fell into the sea and created havoc? Did the dinosaurs wandering these sand flats on that day understand their lives and the world had just changed?

A haunting spectacle of sun and moon, rocks from outer space, light and dark—whether from solar or lunar eclipse, bright daylight with the world in full view or shadowed moonlight with the world in the play of the imagination—we live in light and dark. It is our own minds that bring this alive. How often do we appreciate, or even see, this strange reality? It is there every day and every night. This huge lump of rock called Earth stays on its path and circles the star called the Sun. The rocks shift around, change, evolve. The life on Earth shifts around, changes, evolves. Day after day, year after year. We cannot change what happens but we can watch it, try to understand it, be part of it—the miracle called Earth and life on Earth.

LISTENING FOR TIME

Silence is the beginning of wisdom.
Will Durant

There is no death! The stars go down
To rise upon some other shore,
And bright in heavens jeweled crown
They shine forever more.
John Luckey McCreery

I STOOD ON THE ridge looking down into the canyon. Raising my eyes, I could also look in every direction and see miles to distant horizons—the mountain walls to the east and south, the fading mesas and plateaus to the north and west. I was looking at a scene that evoked feelings of freedom, remoteness, scenic beauty.

Yet, I was not far away from a civilization that teemed below where I stood, erasing that remoteness in a flurry of human activity. But even that strip of modified life stretching mostly along the rivers sat amidst the wildness, not far away from its primeval purity.

I smiled as I thought of what lay hidden in the distance: rushing streams and rivers, deer and elk and moose roaming the forests and meadows, bighorn and antelope foraging the deserts and canyons. This was the West and it indeed was wild and free, belonging to all of us.

But as I gazed through the distant haze under a cloud-dotted blueness that stretched into another direction towards the stars above, I turned my attention to the sounds. Sounds of a distant silence, broken by the wind. I listened.

I tried to hear the call of the soaring condor, once lord of the skies. I have heard that occasionally a condor wanders this way from the canyons to the south and west. I looked and listened, but there were none. Wildlife biologists have diligently tried over the past few decades to save them from extinction and have even extended their wings to new places, but it is a losing battle. I fear their time was in the past. They belong to an age now gone.

I tried to hear the wail of the smilodon—the saber-toothed cat that roamed the plains and mesas, seeking food among the teeming wildlife that were here not that long ago. He is gone, along with the giant bison and the ground sloth and wild native horse, which originated in North America.

I listened for the thunder of the pounding of the tree-trunk-like feet of the mammoth and the mastodon of this open land, south of the glacial mass to the north. They were here not that long ago, now gone forever.

I looked down at the sandstone bedrock at my feet, a rock that sometimes hides the footprints of stegosaurus and allosaurus, the thundering terrible lizards who roamed a swampy and jungle-like world, present now only in the rock that underlies this current world. I will never hear the sounds they made, but I can imagine and pretend.

I listened and heard only the wind—carrying atoms once part of dinosaur molecules, but no living creatures. I heard instead the raven croaking as she soared overhead, the call of the chickadee flitting among the pinyon, and the scuffling of the small lizard chasing crickets under the rocks. I smiled as I thought of the theory that the feathered fliers are descended from the huge and terrifying allosaurus. Maybe I was hearing some echoes from the big guy after all.

This land now was affected by me and my kind. We built roads and trails, set aside areas to keep out bulldozers and houses, cut trees and dug things out of the ground. We are now caretakers of a world that stretches far beyond what I could see. I knew what was out there, but I came here to look for a world long gone. I wanted to see a glance of it, to listen to the sounds it made, marvel at the life that once lived right here.

One of my favorite sayings comes from Ecclesiastes: "Men may come and go, but Earth abides." That is similar to what the Arapaho, Lame Beaver, in James Michener's *Centennial* said: "Only the rocks live forever."

Both seem true, but neither carries the reality of the Earth. Earth changes and even the rocks erode into sand and dust. Given enough time—and time is the winner in all contests—cycles and circles change even the unchanging.

The rocks and cliffs of the NCA as well as the surrounding mountains seem permanent and solid. But look at the canyons. Listen to the flowing water, from river to small stream. Feel the wind as it blows off the cliffs and highlands. See the muddy streams of spring melt and the biting dust of the March windstorms, blowing the dust of Utah and sometimes China past our faces.

The rocks do not live forever. The granite of the inner canyons erodes away, grain by grain. The sandstone of the red cliffs dissolves in the fierce August thunderstorm and the melting January snows. The Earth abides only in the sense that it rises and falls, folds and dives under the mountains, erupts from the seafloors. The Earth is atoms of carbon and iron, nitrogen and silicon, floating in the cosmos since supernovas created them from elemental hydrogen billions of years ago. They constantly rearrange themselves into granite, sandstone, dinosaurs, humans. Oceans of water and oceans of air use them like tinker toys or Lincoln logs. Earth abides only in a basic form that we cannot live long enough to recognize.

So what do we do if we cannot rely on something eternal? We continue as if the rocks *are* eternal. They are for our short lifetime. They are the Earth as are we. If Earth abides, then we do as well.

Again, I closed my eyes as I stood on the rim of the canyon. I listened as the wind flowed off the higher plateau, carrying the cool fresh fragrances of wildflowers, coyotes, streams, and forests of spruce and pine. I saw the far-off oceans. I heard something. Maybe—that might have been the cry of the smilodon after all. Or wait—was that the thunderous roar of the brontosaurus? The sound waves are still circling the earth, carried by the wind that never ends. If only I could hear more clearly through the silence of time.

But life does go on, in cycles and circles. The people who appeared not that long ago probably understood this in a simple way. I wonder if my kind does. We think we own this land, but it owns us. The life that was once here also owns this. It will change and will be here long into the future. And we are just along for the ride. In a broader sense, Earth does indeed abide.

FEMALE RAIN

All rivers run to the sea, yet the sea is not full.
Unto the place from whence the rivers come,
thither they return again.
Ecclesiastes 1:7

THE LAST WEEK of September brought a day of rain. Much needed rain in this desert country. It was possibly the last widespread rain before the soon-to-be snows of fall and winter took over the high country, slowly easing down into the canyons.

Rain comes in two forms according to some of the original inhabitants of this arid West: *female rain* and *male rain*. Male rains come during the summer months, accompanied by wind and lightning. They often come as cloudbursts of heavy rain, much of it immediately running off the rock and cliff ledges, joining surging streams and flash flooding washes. This rain is fierce, quick, and powerful. It helps soothe a dry land, but doesn't last long.

Female rains are the soft, gentle, steady drizzles and light rains that soak into the dry soils, feeding the roots of trees and grass and the foods the ancients tried to grow in this demanding climate. Female rains come in on low-lying, heavy clouds that sink over the clifftop rims, and drop into the canyon bottoms, covering everything with a hazy, grey curtain. Rock walls disappear, high peaks fade into the low clouds, trees play peek-a-boo with wisps of rain and fog. Female rains are the soothing pianissimo violin melody that softens the world into comfort and calm. They contrast with the booming bass orchestral fury of the male rains.

Soon to come this time of year are the snows of deep winter. They are the security blanket that means sleep and a time out from the hectic life of a desert year. On the coldest days, the melting drops of water seep into cracks and fissures of the rock, turning to ice which then slowly picks away and chips out rock and grains of sand from the cliff walls. This patient sculptor re-creates the canyon walls, so gently and slowly we don't notice. But on this September day, the sculptor is yet to come in the never-ending cycles of male and female rain, snow and ice. They are all water, the life force in this arid land.

The deer and the bighorn sheep wander through the canyons as if nothing were different. Coming in and out of the clouds and fog, they are apparitions who belong here. They know where the water is, whether from male or female rain, snowmelt, or springs.

Water always calls to the dusty traveler in this land. A day of female rain calls you out to dance with your arms in the air, waving to the clouds, thanking them for releasing the slow and gentle rain. A day of male rain tells you to take cover, watch the downpour, listen to the thunder roll from cliff-to-cliff, flashing brilliance with the power and danger of the lightning.

A day like this is also a day to sit by an indoor fire, contemplate, take stock, prepare for the hot and dry days that seem to overpower much of the rest of the year. It is a day when you know that life is good and it will continue. The ground soaks up the bounty just as you soak up the feeling that your life-giver is taking care of you. The female rain takes care of you as the mother takes care of her young.

As the clouds started thinning, marking the end of the storm, blue sky and sun slowly broke through the grey cover. Rain dogs—wisps of cloud fragments torn from the sky—hang over the cliffs and mesas. Drifting up and down, sideways one way and then the other, these ragged remnants clung to the cliffs and slopes. Then, a small patch of blue struggled to tear into the gray and white blanket, widening, then disappearing as clouds moved more quickly. Soon, the main blanket of clouds was gone, water still dripped from tree branches, but the steady rain was over. Sun and blue sky would retake their domain and life would go on. The female rain was over for now, awaiting that time when once again, life would reassert itself with its life-nourishing drink from the heavens.

Now the ground steamed as the newly fallen water began its slow journey back into the heavens. Rocks dried, streams slowly fell, now muddied with the red soil and rock. Water is always on the move, from ocean and trees, evaporating to form new clouds. Gentle puffs of clouds drifting past on clear blue sky afternoons, or as male and female storms that release the water to once again pass through the soil, over the rock, down the streams and rivers. A cycle even older than the ancient rocks in these canyons.

Campfire Sky

The night is bright with a starlit sky.
I sit and think as time passes by.
Oh starry night, with a moonlit sky,
take me away and tell me why.
I sit and think all night.
Oscar Wilde

I SAT BY THE campfire, warming myself in the cool night air. What a change from the heat of the day, only a few hours earlier. That happens in these high elevations. I was in the upper end of Big Dominguez, sheltered by pinyon and juniper and enjoying the down-canyon breeze coming off the Uncompahgre Plateau to the west.

The lingering twilight still painted the northwest horizon a pale blue-violet, faded from the brilliant crimson and vermillion of an hour before. Daylight is slow to fade into darkness this time of year.

Countless dots of light continued to paint the darkening sky. I let the fire die to embers so I could enjoy the dark of the crescent-moon sky. Soon only a red glow remained of the fire. It was time now to cast my eyes skyward. I was inspired by the sight of stars and galaxies beyond counting. At the same time, I was disappointed that very few people ever see such a sight. For those willing to take this journey, I thought of the universe it opens up. Literally. It was the universe and it was overpowering. People now are tied to the cities, the bright lights of artificial night times. Who sees such a sky dotted with light?

Ah, the lights. Each dot was either a star in our galaxy or a larger galaxy in the unmeasurable depths of the universe. I've always been fascinated by the meaning of time and space in a view like this. Our ancestors may not have understood things like light years and the billions of star clusters we call galaxies, but surely they felt their insignificant place in this universe. Not knowing what we now call science, they turned to their gods and rituals to give them comfort.

Where did I find my comfort as I felt the warmth of the dying embers at my feet? I heard a coyote singing to his companions from the mesa-top to the north. The cries were mournful, yet they signified the life that goes on day-to-day, season-to-season in this wilderness. The crickets and other night sounds filled the air with a soothing symphony to my ears. If there was anyone else within miles, I had no evidence of it. A setting like this frightens and terrifies many people nowadays, and for some it takes us back to the comfort of a challenging past. We would not be able to count on the comforts we've built for ourselves in the modern overcrowded world. We are losing the ability to enjoy the comfort as well as the danger of a wild setting that belonged to our distant ancestors.

There is danger out there under this spotted blackness of a sky. It is the danger of the life evolved on this planet over eons. The coyotes roaming the plateaus, the cougars prowling the canyons, the bear further up on the mesas— all these belonged here. I was not sure I did. I had lost the confidence, and more importantly, the physical stamina, to roam the canyons by myself.

But I hadn't lost the curiosity, the inspiration to be gained by sitting here under the endless sky. I marveled at the points of light above my head. How many people or beings were up there looking at my galaxy and wondering about any form of life out there? They couldn't see me nor my dying campfire, nor even my planet that contains all I know. If there is intelligent life, what is it like? Does it live in a world anything like mine? Where the higher life forms overpowered all other life, then slowly destroyed what made the life possible?

One of the founding concepts of the wilderness movement was to be able to go back in time, to when we were an integral part of our world. We set aside areas like this to sit in by a campfire and look at an unpolluted night sky. Where we could wonder what was out there making noises in the surrounding forest. Where we could know that what we were seeing was very close to what our distant ancestors could see. And fear. Fear shouldn't be part of this experience, but in a true wilderness, fear added to the joy of being. True to the concept of yin and yang, we had to fear the dark so we could thrill to the light of daytime. Shiver in the chill night air before we could bask in the heat of the canyon day.

For some, a campfire with blazing branches, cut with an axe, embellished with a forked willow stick and hot dogs and s'mores, is a treat to be savored. For me, sitting alone by the small fire—started with one single match and a clump of dead pine needles, then tenderly fed with small branches—gave me time to think. The blaze of the fire itself, dancing yellow with flashes of red, cast an eerie glow that bounced shadows off me and the trees beyond. No need for ghost stories. Ghosts were sitting next to me enjoying the crackling and popping of the fire. Did the passing deer smell the smoke and turn the other way? Did the prowling cougar smell me and slink closer to see what I was?

I was safe by the fire. The darkness of the sky, sprinkled with twinkling dots, the darkness of everything else behind me, all this added to my comfort of the dancing fire light. Wilderness was indeed a state of mind, regardless of the line on a map. I carried my own wilderness within me. It was in every cell in my body, fed by the DNA that held memories of long ago. I realized I didn't belong here, as much as I wished I did. I would return to my world soon, but I let the darkness and the hoot of the great horned owl feed my need to experience what it once was like.

THE FAWN

I WAS WALKING IN the backcountry, exploring the spring blooms and new growth, although on this June day, spring was already a memory in this lower country. I almost stepped on a newborn fawn. I had to look carefully to see if it was even alive. It was so still, not a muscle moved. She finally blinked her large liquid brown eyes, so I knew she was just doing what a long history of instinct required her to do. Mama was close by but junior knew to stay perfectly still while mama got a few minutes to herself. I could see the fur still showing signs of the birth, dried by now, but surely not more than a few hours old.

The fawn had perfectly formed hooves, the large eyes, distinct spots, and that helpless look, although she still would not move a muscle. I carefully backed away, not wanting to disturb things even more. I knew a newborn fawn has no odor, so her behavior would protect her from prowling coyotes or other things that would find her attractive. As I moved further away, I looked closer for mama but still saw nothing. I returned an hour later and no sign of her, so I wished her well, a newcomer to this world.

Spring is the time for new life, be it a deer fawn or juniper seedling or cactus. I wandered over to a rock wall, shaded from the slowly heating air of the dry June day, and sat down. The fawn made me think of what life involves. New life springs up and grows. Some die quickly, but enough survive to keep things going. Old things, whether deer or trees, must die in order to make room for new life. I have always agreed with the saying that nature is amoral. There is not good nor bad, sad nor happy. Life is just there in all its diversity and purpose. We grow attached to the living and despair over the dying, but it is one complicated circle and web, interrelated beyond our understanding.

The fawn will either survive these first dangerous hours and days, or die. The strongest make it, the weaker do not. We are in the midst of a long-running experiment called life that has been going for as long as Earth has been spinning through space around the sun. Life has started, stopped, and evolved from the bacteria that lived in the early seas represented by the rocks at the base of some of these cliffs. It progressed to dinosaurs, then birds and mammals. It is still progressing, to what purpose we wonder and debate. We interject our philosophies, our religions, or spiritual beliefs, try to come to some understanding, but it is a continuing circle, a cycle of change and adaptation.

Deer have probably been around longer than my kind. They have changed, adapted, lived and died. The fawn will continue something that is beyond my comprehension. It doesn't ask the questions I do, or if it does, there is no way for me to know. We sometimes think our kind is the top of the circle since we ask these questions, but as I looked into the big brown eyes of that newborn fawn, I realized she was my equal. Maybe better—could I survive as well as she may, given similar circumstances?

I continued my journey up the canyon. I looked around for a doe, but saw no signs, other than an occasional hoofprint in the dry soil of the trail. This lower country is winter range, providing food and shelter for many deer during the long and dark winter days. What if I ran into a coyote pup, frisking and playing with its siblings, watched by a mother just as cautious and protective as the doe? The coyote wants to eat the fawn. The coyote pups need food and nourishment just as much as the fawn needs her plants. She is a vegetarian; the coyote is a carnivore. Who is better? Who should survive? Both can, but often both don't. Do I pick sides?

Once, while hiking in the redwoods of California, I came across a small patch of thousands of redwood seedlings. There were way too many to survive. Most had to die in order for a few to live to maturity. Recently, a wild turkey hen roamed around my home with her brood of nine. Two weeks later, mama hen made her usual rounds, but with only one chick following. What happened to the rest? I felt sad, but not all can survive. Nature won't let them.

So it was with the fawn I saw. Maybe she will make it, maybe not. The canyons and the rocks don't care. I do. Does that make me special? No. It means the world I would like to see doesn't exist. Nature is amoral. It can be happy as a newborn fawn testing out its legs. Or as happy as three tussling coyote pups wearing thin the patience of mom. Or it can feed the fawn to the pups, or it can starve the pups after mom gets eaten by a cougar.

What does all this mean? It means we live in a complex world that is a fantastically interrelated web of life. We are part of it. We can observe it, listen to it, play on it, float its rivers, hike its trails and enjoy what we have. Sometimes we can manipulate it, control it, even destroy it. It is up to us. But whenever we can, we can try to understand it and appreciate it. Deer fawns as well as coyote pups.

BIGHORN

One does not meet oneself
until one catches the reflection
from an eye other than human.
Loren Eiseley

WE WERE HEADING out of Escalante Canyon when I noticed the big ram just above the road. He was almost a full curl desert bighorn, the prize of the canyons. Above him in the rocks, blending in with the light brown of the dirt and cliffs, were over a half dozen more sheep. A few three-quarter curls stood staring at us. We stopped and started taking pictures. I think they were used to this since they watched nonchalantly in their rather arrogant way. They are powerful, magnificent, and belong here. A symbol of the desert and of wildness itself, they are the caretakers of the canyons, watching over the spirits of those who have come before.

The desert bighorn, a subspecies of *Ovis canadensis*, shares the western half of Colorado with its cousin the Rocky Mountain bighorn, state animal of Colorado. Once the most common animal our ancestors depicted on their panels of rock art, the bighorn is a rare sight for the adventuresome hiker or traveler. Those individuals staring at us were tiptoeing among the rocks, moving like slow water searching for a way to silently disappear.

I thanked the sheep as they moved uphill, blending into the rocks, disappearing into the cliffs. We moved on, but my thoughts remained with these magnificent animals. The only thing better, I mused, would be seeing them further into the wilderness, far from this graveled road we were on. They are there, enjoying their solitude in the distant canyons. They move like ghosts, climbing and picking their way up and down the canyon walls. As much as anything else, they represent the freedom, the solitude, the wildness that used to include all this area.

But the concept of wilderness is a new idea. The original inhabitants roaming these canyons and chiseling pictures of bighorns on red rock walls, knew nothing of the concept of wilderness. All this country was their home. They knew every cliff, every stream, every waterhole in this dry country. Wilderness is our civilized concept that identifies some place where we do not seem to belong except in passing through. We value the concept, accepting it as something we are proud of, set aside as a trophy of our generosity. We have come to believe that roads and houses define our world. Others besides the original natives of this land considered it accessible. Think of the mountain men, the trappers and explorers who left the roads and rivers that comprised their world—a world of comfort. When they entered the plains and mountains, the deserts and canyons, they left the comfort that provided safety. They were now on their own, their skills in survival being tested. They blended with that wildness, or else they did not survive. That survival comes natural for something like the animals of this canyon country. The bighorn meant food, clothing, tools to the people who lived here. All animals meant that, and all plants meant something similar. They belonged anywhere and everywhere.

We cannot know for sure what the rock drawings on the red sandstone rock walls mean, but one possibility is that their pictures of bighorn were a way of saying thank you. Thank you and keep safe so we may use your meat, your bones, your hides, your horns. The ancients relied on the sheep, the sheep relied on the plants, the plants relied on the insects. That is the lesson too many of us fail to understand. The ancients were simple people but much more knowledgeable than we are about the sheep, the canyons, the secrets we still search for in this canyon country. We too, should draw pictures to say thank you and keep you, and paste them all over our homes and walls. Maybe then we might belong as did they and the sheep. That is what survival is all about.

The native people no longer live where their ancestors once did. The sheep have hung on and wander among the rocks and cliff walls. Are they searching for the ancients they shared their homes with? They still offer themselves but find only the silence of the canyons. They share the wind with the canyon wrens, the ravens, the rattlesnakes. They know the location of every seep, every water hole in every season. After I watched them climb around for a short while before they silently disappeared, I knew I still needed to learn from them. I need to go deep into the canyon, climb the cliffs, and take notes. I need to observe the sheep and the ravens and learn what they have to offer. But the danger to me is, if I go in and do that, I may not want to come back out. I may wish to wander with the sheep and discover all the hidden secrets that our ancient ancestors knew. Then I would be part of this canyon country and call it home.

This is where all belong, interconnected, relying on each other. How can we learn if we only pass through, thinking we do not belong? We belong as much as the sheep do, but only if we understand what the sheep understand. We value the sheep as symbols as if they are some prize, something unusual to be seen and photographed. I plead guilty to this. I envy them, although their life is difficult. Life should be. Life is birth and death, struggle and survival.

Life changes for us. Does it for the sheep, the ravens, the lizards? Deep in the canyons of Dominguez and Escalante, the world has stayed much the same as it has been for centuries. That is what the concept of wilderness means. These bighorn symbolize that concept. Life goes on with only the slow erosive change of the canyon walls. Meanwhile, life changes for us at lightning speed in the outside world. Can we somehow combine both worlds? That is the purpose and meaning of a place like this. The bighorn is the teacher. We are the students.

FOOTSTEPS IN TIME

Since you are like no other being
ever created since the beginning of time,
you are incomparable.
Brenda Ueland

THE BASIN OF CACTUS PARK near Gibbler Mountain is surrounded by ridges of Morrison Shale and Dakota Sandstone, and mostly underlain by Entrada Sandstone. All mudstone and sandstone—evidence of a shifting seaway from so long ago—it hurts my brain to think of that amount of time. This was the area I viewed several weeks earlier from the Tabeguache Trail higher to the south—a basin that I thought was missing a lot of rock. That part was true. But I was misled by my previous experiences in Colorado Plateau geology.

What I failed to account for—gently and patiently explained by Eric Eckberg, a very knowledgeable BLM geologist who graciously spent a half day ferrying me around the northern sections of the NCA—were the various layers and thicknesses of sedimentary formations found for hundreds of miles around me. For example, the Wingate Formation is hundreds of feet thick in areas of Utah west of here, but is less than 100 feet thick here. And layers found under the Wingate in Utah are missing here.

What does all this mean? To many people, nothing. Rock is rock. Just like a tree is a tree. Or a mammal is a mammal. But I cannot accept that type of thinking. I have a chronic case of curiosity. To me, rock is a textbook of history.

It tells of the Cretaceous Seaway, the Gulf-of-Mexicosized interior sea that stretched from what is now Canada to Mexico, shifted back and forth, deepening and forming shoreline mudflats and swamplands that ended up being various formations such as Dakota Sandstone and Entrada Sandstone and Moenkopi Sandstone and—well, you get the picture. They have various thicknesses and contain various interesting things. Some have ripple marks and petrified raindrops from when they were the sandflats of meandering rivers and streams. Shifting over millions of years, they are thicker here, thinner there.

But they also indicate what lived there. Some contain fossils, of both plants and animals, but what I found with Eric was a footprint, embedded in a flat surface of rock: the three-toed footprint of a long extinct dinosaur. Several in fact. As I stood there contemplating the prints, I had to come to grips with the fact that I was standing on the exact surface where a dinosaur walked millions of years ago. He, or she, walked along a wet and sandy streambed, looking for food, looking for a place to lay her eggs, escaping from some T-Rex-type predator. Right there. Beside where I now stood. And the coincidence was this petrified footprint in a streambed is also in a dry wash, where water still runs.

I asked Eric if we removed all the soil in the flats surrounding this, would we still find footprints. He said probably. The ancient riverbeds meandered, similar to braided streams in Alaska or river deltas such as the Mississippi or other flat areas with streams wandering for possibly miles. There might be footprints, not only of this three-toed beast, but smaller or bigger animals. I so wanted to climb in that time machine I dream about and go back to see what really happened in this very spot millions of years ago.

In the Morrison Formation, sloping up the adjacent hillsides a few hundred yards away, there are most likely dinosaur fossils, the very bones turned to rocks, but also probably a totally different bunch of animals since we are talking millions of years difference. Millions of years. Separated by only a few feet of modern rock. And this is the story of hundreds of thousands of acres in this NCA and adjacent areas.

Footprints in time. Bones in time. Sands in time. Do you have to be a geologist to understand this? It certainly helps, but you start by looking at the rocks. Look at the colors, the texture, the rock itself. Whether it forms ledges and cliffs or erodes easily. What color is it? White or red or purple?

There are millions of footprints and millions of bones turned to rock as time replaced carbon with silicon in bones and trees. Billions of trees and leaves and vegetation slowly turned to coal or oil or natural gas. Life went on right here, unseen by us. But look closely and you may see—when you try—things hidden by time. They may be hidden from our eyes, but they are there. Maybe the bones of our ancestors are buried waiting for the same thing to happen. The soil hides many things as it recycles simple atoms of carbon and oxygen and silicon. Nature is the ultimate recycling center.

But the footprints in the stone. They are imprinted forever until erosion erases them, maybe to expose more. An animal that no longer roams this Earth walked here, living a normal life. He or she stood right here and looked around. Did he sense that sometime in the far future some new beast would stand here and wonder who came before? Of course not. He lived, walked, and died. With his rock-encased bones maybe close by, hidden under some pinyon tree roots, I walked along the dry wash until I found a damp spot in the sand. Then I stood there with my feet making a small indentation. Someday, some new beast may come along and find that print and wonder. Just maybe.

MODERN FOSSILS

We abuse the land because we regard it
as a commodity belonging to us.
When we see land as a community to which we belong,
we may begin to use it with love and respect.
Aldo Leopold

I⟊ IS EASY to focus on the ancient history of this area, contemplating the cliffs and rock layers, the haze of distant time. But there are newer artifacts than the millions-of-years-old rocks, even newer than the thousands-of-years-old petroglyphs and rock shelters. Nineteenth century explorers of the area included not only the settlers and ranchers such as those who once filled Escalante Canyon; there were even more adventurous people than those.

As Eric—my geology mentor from the BLM office—tried to sharpen my understanding of the geology, he also showed me the recent explorations by early miners in the north Cactus Park area. These hardy prospectors who roamed the plateaus and mesas, either on foot or leading their laden burros and mules, knew what they were looking for. They may not have known the difference between Dakota and Entrada Sandstone formations nor the difference between schist and gneiss, but they did know what type of rock held the promise of copper and gold.

Although the area is composed of sedimentary rocks such as sandstone, mudstone, and shale, these rocks are occasionally infused with igneous sills, dikes, and veins. Where these molten rocks seeped up through cracks and faults, they not only melted and fused with the adjacent sandstone, they cooled and hardened into granitic layers. This is where the old timers knew to look for copper or other minerals. Eric and I explored areas where miners dug and poked around, leaving evidence of their presence: rusted cans and equipment parts and level spots where they cleared away trees and dug into the rock. Old shafts and adits have been filled in for safety reasons, but evidence is still there.

I learned that the depth or width of the fault and resulting vein determined what mineralization occurred. Even though the old-timers may not have understood the science of rocks, they were very adept at following the veins and looking for new ones. Following the one small vein near Farmers Canyon, Eric told me how these veins continued on into Unaweep Canyon to the north, and south to Escalante Canyon. The amount of copper or other ores depended on the characteristics of the veins. How did the old miners, often illiterate of such scientific details, know this? They figured it out by success and failure.

I asked if there was a connection to the vast mineral deposits of the San Juan Mountains not that far to the south. Eric shrugged and said maybe. There is only so much even the experts can know for sure. Their realm is underground and goes back in time as far as the dinosaurs, and much farther. There is a lot of guessing and extrapolation.

For example, when I pressed Eric on the origins of the unique Unaweep Canyon, he once again shrugged. A lot of disagreement among the experts on that one. When I further pressed on why one outcrop of granite sat adjacent to the ancient gneisses or schists, I got the first of several answers "that's just the way it is." Unsaid was the hint to quit asking so many *why* questions.

Prospectors roamed like ants throughout the mountains

of Colorado in the late 1800s. They spread from the mineral-rich zones east and south of the Uncompahgre to this area. I think of them as desperate, expanding into the poor suburbs from the rich cities, but some may have eked out a living. There were no large mines in this vastness, so none really hit it big, but then the pioneer ranchers in nearby Escalante Canyon didn't exactly prosper either.

There is also the evidence of these unfulfilled dreams: rusted machine parts, tin cans, wood structures and rotted beams lie scattered and slowly returning to the earth. Even the old fences, corrals, and house foundations in Escalante Canyon give evidence of past human attempts to tame the wildness. As nearly always happens in these situations, given enough time, nature and the wildness will win eventually.

We find these modern fossils and think about the struggles of our recent ancestors. Their lives were tough and uncomfortable. Now, we race across the flats and hills on bicycles, motorcycles, ATVs, four-wheel drives. We easily carry our comforts with us—food, drinks, folding chairs, cell phones. This is now our playground. While you are playing, think of the miners and ranchers struggling in the heat of the dry August days. Maybe your discarded beer can or candy wrapper will become a treasure to a future explorer. Then again, take it home, let them search a little deeper, they might find something even better.

CIRCLES OF TIME AND ROADS

Wherever we are, it is but a stage on the way to somewhere else
and whatever we do, however well we do it, it is only a preparation
to do something else that shall be different.
Robert Louis Stevenson

I HAVE WRITTEN PREVIOUSLY about circles and cycles. Life and everything else in the entire cosmos goes in circles and cycles. The same in the NCA—the rocks, the life, the physical appearance of the land—can be described in circles and cycles. I also want to describe the routes to circle and travel through the NCA.

I see the network of roads around and through the NCA as a spiderweb of interconnected opportunities. Although a large chunk in the middle is designated Wilderness, the interwoven series of roads and paths around the perimeter ties the whole together.

You can drive paved roads along the east and north sides, taking you from the very south edge to the northern edge. Both are bounded by canyons: Unaweep to the north, Cottonwood to the south. Cottonwood is inaccessible other than by hiking down cross-country to this straight-as-an-arrow small canyon. The Unaweep's walls surround and tower over the highway, providing an enigma to geologists on how and when it all formed. It is a mini-Yosemite, with no current river or stream going its full length. As a matter of fact, it is unique in that streams originate in the middle of the canyon, and run towards each end. Strange, indeed.

Off these two paved highways run several major

graveled roads that lead through the area and along its western edge. Escalante Canyon is the major easy access into the area and it offers the best automobile access into the heart of the canyon-walled wonderland. It is famous for its history of pioneer settlers, with hints of a rough and tumble beginning. For earlier residents, their history lies hidden with the echoes of the canyon wren on the red rock walls.

Sawmill Mesa Road (except for a few bedrock stretches), 25 Mesa Road, and the Divide Road along the spine of the Uncompahgre Plateau, are good graveled roads that connect via the spiderweb of more rugged and rocky dirt roads and paths that remain from early cattle and mining access.

You can navigate from one to another, often with long treks across seemingly endless grass and forest of the Uncompahgre Plateau highlands, of which the NCA is a small bottom section. The Plateau is massive and any serious exploration of the entire area needs days. Whether by car, truck, bicycle, or ATV, the views change from trail to trail. The expanse of Gibbler Gulch as seen from the Tabeguache trail is impressive, offering the wide-open views of western Colorado and a preview of eastern Utah. The steady uphill climb of Sawmill Mesa on the southern edge offers previews of the larger plateau to the west. When the driving or pedaling gets tiring, the opportunities for hiking, floating, and exploring by foot or even hoof are as endless as the Plateau itself.

I have talked about the time displayed in the rocks. This area is about time. But time to explore and drive seem almost as limitless. As seen from the east, the Uncompahgre Plateau is the beginning of the Colorado Plateau, although truth be told, some of the rock formations of the Colorado Plateau do sneak a ways east of here, even to the Front Range across the Continental Divide. Most of the sedimentary formations plentiful west of the main Rockies have long since been eroded away as the Rockies rose to their present heights. Rock layers were being laid in Jurassic and Triassic swamps and seas before the Rockies rose to their cloud-bumping heights. But the rising granite lifted those rocks high enough to be eroded to nothing in the time spans involved.

Many of the roads in this area originated as deer or sheep trails long before our human ancestors filtered into the area from places unknown. They followed easy access and usually led the way to water. Early humans often used the same trails, maybe veering here and there for convenience. They also looked for water, but took advantage of the game as they followed and hunted the animals. Then the early paths were used by modern humans as we enlarged them for our evolving means of travel. Wider for horses, then horse-drawn wagons, then vehicles, larger and larger. Purposes of access changed, from hunting, to looking for minerals, moving cattle, and traveling for pleasure and challenges as new technology gave us newer vehicular toys.

Once we realize we can get around to see the NCA, we can then contemplate the circles and cycles of the area itself. Time is one of my favorite subjects and it is something very few really understand, including myself. Time is not about reading a watch or looking at a calendar. Those measures can give an indication of our perspective but do not define time. As I stand looking at the cliffs of Dominguez and Escalante canyons, I can see the results of time. Time long past. I can look up into the sky during a new moon and see into the future, a time yet to come. The universe is old but there is still much happening and we can visualize the changes as old stars die and explode, creating the dust for new stars and solar systems to coalesce from nothing into something.

We can see the same thing here as we view the results of time gone by: when ancient seas covered the area, when ancient rivers flowed into mudflats and river deltas, when lava oozed from vents and volcanoes to the east and south. A different time when creatures that no longer exist roamed the very rock I am now standing on. A time when sand deserts that stretched beyond the horizon blew red sand that after a long time turned into red cliffs of hard sandstone. Our trails and roads climb up out of canyons that were carved over time as the same river I now watch rolls by on its way to the ocean, and its smaller streams cut and carved these magnificent canyons that are now only echoes of what once was.

Time is something that connects us with former lives. The very atoms that make up our bodies and minds hold a memory of that time. The hydrogen and oxygen, calcium and iron are made of atoms that are made of electrons and protons that are made of quarks and mesons and who knows what else that may just be nothing but pure energy. And that energy once helped shape this land and carve the canyons, left footprints in the rock and fossilized bones in the Cretaceous muds of time long ago.

Just as the roads on the surface connect in circles, the time that makes up this land goes in circles as well. We just happen to stand or drive or ride along, looking at trees and cactus and rocks and rivers and think of the past, the present, and the future. This land will change, new types of birds will fly over, new canyons will eat into the mesa tops, new trees will grow and die and we will become the ancient past.

It is too much to contemplate as I figure out which road to take next. What new serendipities will I find? Can I see the circles of life that surround me? I am part of it. What is the past and what is the future? The present is so short-lived; the future becomes the past almost instantly as the present lasts about as long as the quarks that pop in and out of existence in this quantum universe.

Time. How do we spend the short blink of an eyelid

amount of time we have in our own lives? Every end marks a beginning. The end of the sea muds of the Chinle formation began the dry desert sand dunes of the Wingate. The end of the Tabeguache/Bridgeport Road marks the beginning of the trail up Big Dominguez. The end of Escalante Forks marks the beginning of the climb to Bennetts Basin. You circle around the NCA and you circle back in time to catch up to the present, then contemplate the future. You can make the choices. The land is connected by roads, paths, and trails. The land is also connected as part of time. Plan your time well.

BALM FOR THE SOUL

He who wants to have right without wrong,
order without disorder, does not understand
the principles of heaven and earth.
Chuang Tzu

THE SUMMER OF 2017 had exhausted me with the abundance of discouraging news. From terrorists to weather disasters and general discord, it seemed one disaster after another was sapping my energy. I needed positive energy. I had to get away and reconnect with the good we live amongst.

I escaped to Escalante Canyon, which was rapidly becoming a favorite place for me to breathe in peace and goodness, from the blue sky down to the red cliffs and granite inner canyon. My first stop was to find a whispered secret petroglyph panel on the small cliffs near the boat ramp. I easily found them, only yards away from a dirt road. I scrambled up the scree of boulders and cactus. I stood next to the carvings: people, deer, bear paws, and other scratchings that neither I nor anyone else will ever know fully what they mean. Thankfully they weren't ravaged by vandals.

I looked for long minutes at the drawings, soaking in the deep peace they represented, to me at least. I turned and looked down at the river. I tried to envision what the people would have seen the day or days the drawings were made. How many decades or centuries ago did that happen? They wouldn't have seen the railroad, the gravel road with new concrete bridge, the ranch houses and buildings, and the field of old vehicles on the far hillside. They would have seen water slowly flowing down a willow- and cottonwood-lined riverway between towering cliffs. There was no negative thinking here, except maybe for thoughts of killing a rabbit or deer for supper. But that was a necessary and peaceful kill, if there can be such a thing.

I drove up canyon, the peaceful and calming energy increasing as the cliffs rose from the canyon floor—the white and tan sandstones replaced by the red Wingate, and the red-purple Chinle, the mudstone that lies atop the granites of the inner gorge. My knowledge of the sedimentary formations is clouded by what I learned in southern Utah; the formations change as they creep eastward to the Uncompahgre.

Seeing cottonwoods lining a small canyon originating in the northern wall of the main canyon, I began hiking up the drainage to find the source. I knew springs seeped out of the Wingate on the north wall and I followed a dry streambed that turned moist, then flowed with water. I struggled through the narrow streambed, fighting thickets of oak brush, sumac, cattail, sedge, deep ravines, and house-sized sandstone boulders. Finding the going nearly impossible along the creek, I slowly climbed uphill, only to find huge boulders, dead and down trees and branches, and more deep ravines again hindering progress. This may not have been official *wilderness*, but it might as well have been. Truly an oasis in the desert, this secluded side canyon offered a challenge but also a reward. Seeps lined the north cliff, with dampness exuding from the contact between Wingate and Chinle. Monkeyflowers clung to the rocks, with columbines thick in the damp soil beneath. White calcium carbonate stains covered the wall indicating a long history of seepage.

I finally gave up my quest to find the main headwall spring; the tangle of boulders and vegetation ending my efforts on this hot day. I didn't mind as I sat in the shade of a huge boulder to eat lunch. The red cliffs across the narrow canyon were topped by white cumulus clouds. I called to see if any canyon wrens were nearby; sure enough, one answered me from far up the towering walls to the north. That sound was enough to dissipate any lingering thoughts of the unnerving outside world. This inner world in the secluded side canyon was in full peace. I was tucked away and protected by the red rocks and green wetland grasses and thickets of oak, sumac, sedges and cattails. This was the sanctuary I was seeking.

I could have sat there all day, but further exploration called. In my scrambling down the talus slope, clambering over huge red boulders, I found slabs of rock that were crumbling into paper-thin sheets of sandstone. I wanted to take a thin sheet home, but whenever I peeled it off the parent rock, it crumbled in my hands. It belongs up here, after all, I thought. It would feed the sandy creek bottom as the grains started their long journey to the sea.

After returning to my vehicle, I thought I would try one more side canyon. Once again, I followed the cottonwoods as they snaked up the drainage, soon lining a stream that flowed water from hidden springs. Once again, I was stopped by the thicket of vegetation. So I climbed high up, and again was stopped by house-sized boulders at the cliff base. I was not dismayed like I might have been on another day. I didn't mind that my destination was not reached. On this day, I knew the journey itself was the goal. The objective was not to locate the source of the creek. This was a journey of finding peace in a turbulent world, and I found it. The towering cliffs, puffy white clouds, singing birds and flowing water in this hidden canyon were the balm I needed.

My final stop for the day was at the Potholes, to peer over the edge at the main Escalante stream far below, winding through the granite inner gorge. Even that turbulent little stretch of stream seemed peaceful on this day, although

I knew it was a force that never stopped in its relentless grinding away of the hard rock below. I didn't focus on the force and power, but on the steady progress of a never-ending goal. The stream looked peaceful, compared to what I saw back in April—a raging power that ravaged the solid rock walls grain by grain.

If I hadn't worn myself out trying to climb up the two side canyons, I would have scrambled down to the creek and soaked in the pools. It was sufficient to stand up on the granite boulders and look down upon the peaceful stream as it wound towards the Potholes past where I stood. The day was complete. I could return to the crazy world outside this protective canyon, knowing where to come whenever I need peace.

SOLITUDE

Not until we are lost do we begin
to understand ourselves.
Henry David Thoreau

DRIVING WEST FROM Delta, I started up the long easy grade called Sawmill Mesa. Not a true mesa, but a long, sloping plateau, a sagebrush and pinyon-juniper-dotted expanse bordered by two large canyons falling off on either side. Cottonwood Canyon on the south and Dry Fork Escalante Creek on the north were hidden from view past the flat tabletop of Sawmill Mesa. While driving, all you see is the flatness and the bedrock that paves the road in places. Like other areas on the larger Plateau, the road seems to go on forever.

After a short jaunt on national forest lands to the west, the road that goes ever on turned north and I came upon a viewpoint overlooking Escalante Forks far below. Of the many views I have been coming across in my journeys, this is one of the very best. Spread out to the west are the headwaters of several of the Escalante Forks. Hidden by another mesa is the main Escalante. The red rock walls of Wingate sandstone slowly dive into the protective cover of the Uncompahgre highlands. This gently undulating green carpet slopes further on up to the top of the Plateau. It reminds me of blocks of Carrera marble that Michelangelo prepared in order to release the *David* or *Pieta* hidden inside. The red rock cliffs continue on under the carpet, waiting to be uncovered in the future. This is the same with the other table-top mesas and canyon rims. They hide the cliffs underneath, waiting to see the light of day for the first time in millions of years.

People usually explore this country with friends or family. To fully appreciate the scenery and the land itself, I suggest seeing this country alone. As I sat on the edge of Dry Mesa further east, I was overlooking Tatum Draw, one of the minor side canyons leading to the main Dry Fork. With only broken rock for soil, scattered pinyon and juniper, and a few clumps of small plants, I was alone with the view. Total silence overwhelmed me. As far as I knew, there were no people within miles, and with my back to the road, I saw no evidence of humankind anywhere. This is the type of solitude that opens the soul to creative thought. I wondered why there were lines of rock cliffs interspersed with sloping talus. A line of cliffs of Dakota sandstone, then a slope, then the reds and purples of Morrison, then broken boulders all the way down to the canyon floor. Horizontal lines dominated the landscape. Rock—pure Mother Earth— rules the landscape.

This could have been the type of view seen by the Hebrew prophets three thousand years ago in another part of the world. Those views may have helped open them up to their insights and creativity. A sere rocky landscape colored with tans and browns and reds, topped by a blue sky. And at my feet the sculpted twisting forms of grey juniper trunks and branches of trees long dead. They persist in keeping guard over a world long gone, just as the lichen-covered cliffs keep watch over a world gone a million times longer. Long past their creation, but they all combine to form the living world I am now part of.

My solitude and slight apprehension of being so alone is different from the people who wandered here millennia ago. They were part of the solitude and belonged here. They may have passed by in their hunt for food or in a journey to new areas, but this land was home. To me, it was a landscape I was visiting but it was not comforting or welcoming. It was far from my home and hostile in a strangely protective way. I was an invader and a stranger.

Still uncertain of the path ahead, having never traveled this road before, I headed east. Soon the road dove off the mesa top and fell in hairpin curves, and a steep, rock-jumbled line down the cliffs. Nervous about heading down a road I was not comfortable having to come back up if I had to, I headed down in granny four-wheel drive. This reminded me of forays into the Moab, Utah, backcountry. Surrounded by rock cliffs and canyons, that jumbled red rock country further west offers a slightly more comfortable form of solitude, mainly because the solitude is not as remote as this Escalante country. Still, I was only a few miles from a more crowded civilization than Moab. What was the difference? Discomfort with the unknown held me in suspense in Dry Fork. I knew people at that very moment were crawling the roads near Moab, with someone nearby. Solitude comes in many forms.

Finally reaching the stream at the bottom—running with a slight flow of muddy water from recent rain—I breathed a sigh of relief as I knew I was close to home and could make it easily from this point on. But the experience lingered in my mind. This was one of dozens of canyons and side canyons that finger off the higher uplands to the west. Very few have roads or even trails. Most run straight west to east, high elevation to low, all eventually leading to the Gunnison River that leads out of the canyon country.

This is one more example of discovery in a landscape full of surprises. Canyon after canyon, most often running in a straight line west to east, with side canyons edging in. Rock cliff after rock cliff laid bare as the canyons slowly eat away the edges of the flat mesa tops. Without people or vehicles intruding on my meditations, I found a solitude that was so personal, so overpowering, I wanted to hide somewhere. I was alone in a setting so ancient, it spoke volumes to anyone who wishes to listen. It took courage to listen, for the echoes of the past are of an earth violent as well as calm. Solitude can do that. It cares not for the comforts of home and familiarity. It calls to your very soul to think about who you are and where you are going. The breeze of the canyons is trying to call you home. Out here, home is a place you have never been.

THE VIEW FROM ABOVE

Imagine a place on Earth so awesome,
so vast, so pure. We can hardly breathe its air.
Imagine the Earth alive with morning,
shimmering white nights, no end of sky, no end of sea.
Carole Foreman

I HAVE ALWAYS BEEN intrigued by canyons—the rock walls, the shapes of the rockfalls, the seeps and springs, and of course the streams or rivers that created them. But to complete the picture, one needs to make the effort to climb to the rim of a canyon wall. The world changes, opens up, and divulges an expanse that surrounds the canyon itself, hidden by its sheltered view.

I stood on the Escalante Canyon south rim, taking in the view. An hour before, I had been standing in the canyon floor far below. The entire canyon now came into view, with the road and stream at the bottom merely pencil lines of brown and green. Earlier, I was inside looking out, to the colorful rock cliffs and blue sky. But up here, the entire world opens up. The canyon is impressive with its large V-shape, but the rest of the world outside the canyon lies in unending expanse. Far to the north, the Bookcliffs form the horizon north of the Colorado River. Grand Mesa juts its mass into the surrounding valleys. The San Juans to the south, with their white-capped, sawtooth ridges, are the end of the known world visible from here. The West Elks and Ruby Range line the eastern horizon. The Gunnison and North Fork Valleys lie below—green and brown—where civilization huddles in its gentle and flat blanket. And to the west, the broad and nearly flat-topped hump of the Uncompahgre hides the rest of the canyon-riddled Colorado Plateau that makes up half of Utah.

This expansive view dwarfed the canyon, which previously had dwarfed me. As I stared, I thought of the other canyons that lie hidden in this world. There are many that dwarf even this canyon that I think impressive beyond comprehension. The Black Canyon of the Gunnison shelters the river that sliced through a rising mass of granitic rock. Unaweep—a canyon now without a river but hiding secrets of an ancient one—marks the almost-northern end of the Uncompahgre Plateau. Big Dominguez hides just north of Escalante—hidden from any view other than by an eagle—wilderness in its true form. Only eagles and bighorn sheep are comfortable there. And of course, fly over the mass of the Plateau to the west and the "real" canyons of the Colorado River dwarf everything else combined.

Rock. This is a world of rock—reds and oranges, whites and browns. The rock tells a story that humbles any human who stumbles into and out of the canyons that wind through the mesas. I was on top of the mesa and wanted to be back in the comfort of the canyon. Down there, I was one-on-one with the rocks and streams, the pinyon and sagebrush, lizards and canyon wrens. Up here, I can see the rest of the world. I know the expanse of life, the diversity, the problems and opportunities that litter the tangle that is modern life. Down in the canyon, all that is hidden. If I thought of any of it, it was because I brought it in with me. If I could shut it out, I could focus on what lay at my feet and rose above me. That is a level of comfort hard to explain.

As I stood on the rim on this warm spring day—the afternoon winds rising with the swirling thermals dotted with ravens as they rose and played—I thought of what was below me. I was seeing only a fraction of the carved landscape from this eagle perch on the canyon rim. Not the canyon to the north—that was too obvious—but what was beneath my feet. There is a massive canyon below me that has not yet been uncovered. Escalante Canyon might widen, breaking off canyon edges to create a much larger valley. Or a small rivulet might slowly deepen, cutting smaller gullies that will grow into small canyons eventually deepening to the depths I was seeing in the adult canyons. At some time in a future counted in millions and not dozens of years, all this rock will turn to sand and head towards whatever ocean is convenient.

The blue sky looked innocent enough. A few wispy clouds—painted with the mares' tails of a white celestial paintbrush—told of an approaching cold front that might or might not bring rain. But given time, this blue sky will turn grey and blue-black hurling lightning and rain, snow and ice in an endless procession that lets water and gravity melt away even the hardest granite. Canyons, regardless of the rock formation to be removed, are the work of time and water, gravity and wind.

I lowered my eyes to my feet. The horizons felt too expansive, too cosmic. The rock at my feet tugged at my attention like gravity. I was standing high on a mesa of rock and sand, a few clumps of grass, an occasional pinyon tree. Life was indeed simple and time played it like a fine violin. Time and rock and water and gravity. What else is there?

THE RIVER: BEING AND MOVING

You cannot step twice into the same river,
for other waters are ever flowing on to you.
Heraclitus

THE GUNNISON RIVER has a history and a story before it even gets to the Escalante and Dominguez Canyon area. A long time ago, what was later called the Gunnison River left the high mountain meadows and forests and cut its own canyons and valleys before it sliced through the rising granites that later hemmed in the cataracts in a new canyon we then named Black. The rock is black and the foaming and violent water is white as it thunders and surges in a wonderland of rock and space. The space is narrow and tall, before it erupts into the blue sky that covers what lies below—a sky that furnishes the water that carves the canyon.

Leaving the black and narrow-walled canyon, the river still is entrapped in a gorge, surrounded by smaller sandstone cliffs. Our early ancestors camped along its shores, never wondering what it was called, where it came from, or understanding where it would end up. It brought life and sustained it. That was enough to know. The petroglyphs and pictographs spoke to their descendants, or to their gods and gave thanks and may have asked for assistance.

After a slow journey across open desert lands, now converted to corn fields and houses, the river once again enters canyons. Only this time the water skirts the edge of the high plateau to the west, as it wends its way to an even larger river—originally the Grand—but now officially named for the state and the red color of its rocks. Smaller canyons enter from the west, draining the higher land once part of a much higher range. It is once again the sandstones and mudstones that once covered a flatter land or ocean floor. The very rocks of these canyons were formed adjacent to or under water and now rely on water to erode them and move them to the sea.

As the river peacefully winds along the edge of the highlands to the west, it is bounded by red rock cliffs and lined with willow and grass. It gives no hint of the turmoil it had gone through only miles upstream. It is now slowly wending its way north, then west, then south, then west again, unaware of the magnificent canyons and slickrock wonders that lie ahead. It is a journey like none other on this planet, a journey that unwraps the history told through rock and erosion, water and gravity.

The peaceful and tranquil stretch bordering the Uncompahgre canyons is a brief respite, allowing reflection and rest. Once long ago, this same river and maybe the Colorado itself may have turned west to cut through a rising plateau, creating canyon walls that now border no river. The phantom canyon—called Unaweep—now stands sentinel over a past long abandoned. Once, our river may have helped cut this large canyon on a shortcut west, but later gave up this route and went another way. This still remains a mystery, but the river doesn't care where it goes, relentlessly heading downhill, even if that downhill shifts and changes paths. History and time are apathetic beyond measure.

The river, fast and muddy with spring runoff, or slow and clear with late autumn flow, carries its own story and its own life. The fish searching the depths or shallows, the ducks and geese floating the edges, the insects swarming the surface or the sedge-lined banks, all belong here in their own world. It is not our world and we can visit but not belong. The river itself, from high in its snow-capped beginnings, or low where the mudflats merge into the Sea of Cortez, is a place we live along, use relentlessly, dam and remove parts of, but we can never conquer it.

The river represents so many things. It brings and sustains life. It erodes the mountains and carves the canyons. It is ever-changing yet ever the same. It is time and it is timeless. It has been here long before anyone existed who could give it a name and it will be here long after anyone is left who could understand a name.

Not thinking about what this river or the water that flows in it has gone through, we flow along with the current in a boat casting a fishing line hoping for the thrill of snagging a fish. We ride in a rubber raft enjoying the warmth of the sun and the cooling splash of the water. We stand up on a strange looking surfboard as we ride the river. We hunt ducks from the shore. We stand on the shoreline and throw rocks, adding to the pebbles the river is slowly eroding. The river entertains us as it slowly does its work of being and moving. Ice forms along the edges on a frigid January morning. Birds build nests in the willows and grasses on the edges in a warming springtime. Life abounds in, under, on, and next to the flowing water. It is truly a life force but still foreign to us.

This very river was once the highway into and out of this broad valley, the only way past and through glacier-capped mountains. It now shares its path with a railroad and hiking path, and a handful of bridges that cross it. Its murmur is constant, rising and falling with the rainfall and snowmelt. It, and not the rock cliffs, are the constant that flows through time.

As I stand along the banks, I watch its passing, thinking of its journey, past as well as future. I can wade in it, scoop it up. My kind can throw a huge concrete barrier across it and stop it temporarily, but it will win out. It has cut through these rocks, carved canyons, washed away houses and people and lives and will continue to do so for as long as water falls from clouds onto mountains and deserts.

The river does what water always does. It flows downhill until there is no more downhill. Then it spreads out and becomes a world of its own. This river, this flow of water that started as snowmelt and raindrops high along the Continental Divide began a journey that takes it to a distant sea, where it then evaporates and rides the wind back to the mountains in the form of clouds that come as snowstorms and rainstorms, driven by wind and accompanied often by lightning. The mountains reach into the clouds and remove the water, sometimes quietly, sometimes violently. But as long as the mountains have been there, and much longer before that, water has fallen to earth, where gravity then keeps it flowing downhill. It is a cycle that never ends.

IT IS ALL ABOUT THE LAND

We shall not cease from exploration,
And the end of all our exploring
Will be to arrive where we started
And know the place for the first time.
T. S. Eliot

W E MADE OUR annual July 4th outing to take the family portrait, the last, I am sure, for our 14-plus-year-old, arthritic, tri-pawd Aussie/border collie; thus it was special. She enjoyed sniffing the once-familiar scents and fresh mountain air, now beyond her ability to run free in. Even though our photo spot was on the eastern end of Grand Mesa, and off the National Conservation Area by a few miles, it still reminded me of the importance of the land. The setting was different—higher, more lush and green, with aspen and spruce forests mixed with flower-dotted meadows and lakes—but it was not unlike the highlands of the Uncompahgre Plateau, just a few short miles west of the NCA.

Higher in elevation means more rain and snowfall. Which means more water. Which means more vegetation and life. However, I visualized the view from upper Dominguez, looking down-canyon, and imagined that area could have been the very same view I was now looking at, only eons ago. The NCA makes up the eastern edge of the Plateau, which once was a vastly higher mountain range, now eroded down to a modest miles-long bump on the land. It is still high elevation, with aspen and spruce forests and wildflower-dotted meadows. The red rock canyons of the

NCA once may have lain buried hundreds if not thousands of feet below the verdant green uplands such as I stood upon today.

Regardless of whether the country is high alpine, red rock desert, tall grass prairie, coastal redwood rainforest, southern swamp and bayou or eastern oak and maple forest, it is all about the land. We have civilized ourselves to the point of living on the land but not knowing the land, much less appreciating it. The very Earth we live on supports us, feeds us, houses us as we slowly erode our welcome.

It is all about the land. We are part of a system that includes and weaves together so many and so much in a very complex web of life. We are not the end-product or top rung. Although we have the power to destroy and alter and manipulate, we do not, nor will ever have, the power to create. The land is what we inherited and it is all we have or will ever have. How many of us know anything at all about the rock beneath our feet, the trees over our heads, the animals surrounding us?

We have heard many times about the fragility of planet Earth—a spaceship adrift in a large, apathetic universe of time and space. We are all we have. There is no substitute, no replacement to come in and relieve us. The land is all there is.

The NCA is protected by Congressional designation. It is too dry and rocky for any type of farming. It is too rough and remote for houses or even roads. There are no trees to log. It was deemed beyond commercial use, thus set aside as public land, then set aside as wilderness and special treatment. But it does have value if we care to take the time to hear it, to see it, to feel it. Time to sit and stare at the blue sky and red rock cliffs, the cactus flowers and bighorn sheep. This land is part of who we are and who we have been for centuries. It is part of us, even if we rarely venture into the canyons and onto the mesa tops.

On a day like July 4, even if we do not visit it, this land defines the freedom we celebrate. The land can be free, just like its people. The people who lived here for millennia were free, more so than we will ever be. The land is in its natural state, unfettered. It has its own government, its own constitution, its own citizens.

We tend to celebrate many things and many occasions. Each one of us needs to, on a special occasion, sit under a tree, on a rock, at the seashore, on a mountaintop, and listen. Listen to the land and the water flowing over it, the animals running on it or flying above it. Watch the plants growing on it, digging roots deep into the soil, slowly breaking up bedrock to create new soil which will nourish new plants and animals. That is the freedom we should celebrate.

Whether you have driven to a remote location by truck, ridden an ATV, motorcycle or bicycle, hiked in by trail or cross country, or floated on the river, you are in an isolated area of what some may think an endless expanse of arid land. The people who may think this is typical sagebrush plains are missing something valuable. Take a few moments to explore and you will find what they are missing.

Find a cliff wall, a large rock, a weathered and twisted pinyon or juniper, a clifftop overlook, a streamside cottonwood, alder or horsetail patch. Turn off any machine or device that makes noise. Relax and breathe deeply. Breathe in the pine- or sagebrush-scented air, free of exhaust and other man-made smells, other than your own perspiration. As you snuggle up to the rock or tree or ground, close your eyes. Listen to the quiet.

Observe—with your ears, your eyes, your nose, your fingers—what you are now part of. You have become one with something primeval, something as old as Earth itself. You have become part of Earth. Notice the details. See the shapes, the textures, the forms of rock, cliff, tree. Feel the grit of the sandstone, smell the bark of the pinyon, see the veins of the alder leaf, the joints of the prehistoric horsetail plant. Lay your hands on the soil and feel the warmth, see the colors. Watch the lizard as he scurries across the ground. Feel the air lifting the wings of the soaring raven or the flittering chickadee. Notice the texture of the snow-white clouds drifting across the sky.

It only takes a few minutes to become one with a landscape that most people never experience. It only takes a few minutes to become part of an experiment unique in our solar system. As far as we know, nowhere else for countless billions of miles in a vast universe can you meld with life itself in a setting like this. This is a moment in time that will never come again in exactly the same way. Savor the experience. Make a memory that will last a lifetime.

Enter a dream—a dream where you belong in a time and a place. This is the time and this is the place. You will always be able to come back and visit. This is your connection to your home, a sense of place.

We all live a fast-paced life, in a world of noise, crowds, artificial disturbances. When you return to that world, you now carry with you a life-preserver, something you can bring forth in your mind. Return to that moment of quiet, that time you were part of something millions of years old. Reflect on what you felt, saw, heard—the moment your very soul became aware of what is important and what is not. It is a dream, but it is not a dream. It is now a part of you. You carry within yourself a treasure to savor forever. Trust it, honor it, protect it. It is all about the land.

NEVER ENDING JOURNEY

If there is magic in the planet,
it is contained in water.
Loren Eiseley

THE MID-OCTOBER BLUE skies portended a coming storm, wisps of clouds starting to flow slowly over the Plateau. The aspen gold in the high country had long faded and fallen as winter compost. Several light snows had dotted the peaks with white, but the perfect October warmth had melted the white back to autumn brown.

Down along the river, the steady flow of greenish Gunnison water wound between the reds and oranges and golden yellow of the riverbank jungle. Although not by design, I picked the perfect day to float the river. Rooster, the BLM river ranger, was guiding me from Bridgeport to Whitewater in a sleek red Mad River canoe. I had spent days off and on throughout the summer exploring the canyons, the mesas, the expanse of the NCA. I had saved the perfect setting for a perfect ending of my explorations. They of course will not end, now that I have discovered a secret paradise, but autumns usually symbolize endings, so end this adventure I would for now.

Rooster is the epitome I had come to expect of this type of government employee. Knowledgeable beyond his vast experience, he is gentle, informative, and a perfect guide. One of three river rangers, he spends his time in river patrol, caring like a mother doe for his watery kingdom. After I admitted this was my first time in a canoe, he gave me a safety lesson well beyond what we would need today. His years of experience had proven to him there is never too much emphasis on safety on water. And this water on this day was deceptive. The wide river flowed gently and slowly at times, but was still full of hazards for the careless.

We put in at Bridgeport, pushing off past a dead bear lying in the shallows right at the boat launch. Ravens worked away at the ripe-smelling carcass, probably floated down from who knows where. Rooster did say this is bear country, pointing out Russian olives in a nearby island shredded by bear claws. Maybe this bear had lived nearby after all.

The boat launch at this site leaves much to be desired, but options are scarce since the railroad runs right along the river and there really are no other locations than this spot. We carried the canoe under a railroad trestle, careful of the ravine eating away the narrow trail. The river was wide, but surprisingly shallow in spots. The canoe paddle often hit rocks, even in the middle of the easy-going river. As we floated and slowly paddled, we watched a bald eagle land in a large, yellow cottonwood on the west bank. A huge nest was constructed in the cottonwood's upper branches.

A great blue heron watched us float by, then decided we were too close as he lifted off, a lumbering but graceful form that eased downriver, legs dangling. Ducks rose up in a complaining noise far ahead of us. This stretch of river is lonely, with only the railroad along its east bank, and the wilderness to the west. Miles of canyons and mesas hide in the expansive landscape towards the towering Plateau that creates the distant skyline.

As the river winds around a long projection called Tunnel Point, the water flows against massive sandstone cliffs that dive directly into the water, no shoreline here. We beached the canoe on the tall grasses of the west bank, then hiked a short distance to a small canyon entering the expansive piece of private land called Sand Flat. Rooster pointed out pictograph panels. These were obviously recent since they contain horses and figures with rifles—the last message from the Utes before our ancestors kicked them off land wanted for other things. I made a silent apology and once again wondered what the rock scribes were trying to tell me.

We passed several official BLM campsites along the river, shaded by massive ancient cottonwoods, now yellow with the brilliance of the season. They harmonized with the reds and oranges and gold of the willows, grasses and other plants forming a wall of shore vegetation. Grasses well over head-high hid the actual shore, as we found at two places we tried to land.

The river was fast in places, lake-like in others. I would have loved to just float and let the river take us at its pace, but we had to paddle to meet our self-imposed schedule. This was a place that begged me to return, but at the pace of the land itself—slowly, in detail imposed by the rocks and grasses that hide unseen wonders. Except for the almost invisible railroad, then a passing train (with which we exchanged welcoming waves, and understanding that to each of us, we were in a special place), we were passing along the edge of a magical place unknown to most people.

As we floated past Dad's Flat, a piece of private land lined with magnificent old golden cottonwoods (accessed only from Cactus Park to the west), we started seeing small canyons carved through the sandstone wall along the west side of the river. Small side canyons that I knew would hold discoveries worth investigating. "Another time," I sighed, as we paddled across long distances of slack water. Lakes in the river, I commented, and Rooster agreed.

After my summer of explorations of the rock-walled canyons, I thought *the rock* was the ancient thing of this Earth—that the billion-year-old bedrock hidden underneath the newer sandstones was the elder of this Earth. But no, the oldest thing, passing even the oldest rock seen anywhere, is the water. Each drop has been here since the beginning. It has changed form, from water vapor rising from a sea now gone, to the raindrop or snowflake, falling to earth, then flowing as rivulet, stream, river, back to the ocean. The water is old, ancient, giver of life. Without water, the land is the blood red of the Wingate sand desert turned to red cliffs. The land needed water to urge the life from the ocean to the shore, then to the swamps and jungles. All the while, the rock formed and dissolved, always moved by water.

Where was this water taking me? It controlled me; I was at its mercy. If I stayed with it, I would be churned through unmeasurable rapids and falls and canyons before being spit out into the Gulf. Not today. I would leave the water and it would continue on. I will see it again as it falls as snow on the high peaks of the Divide, or in a summer thunderstorm, returning to old canyons and cliffs, bringing life and new canyons. All a part of time, that question I have been searching to find meaning of in this wilderness of rock and sky.

Yes, this river is the answer that underlies all my questions. I sit back and enjoy its life-giving sentience. It is not all about the land. It is all about the water. And this river carries it never ending on its search for a destination, just like me.

PHOTO GALLERY
& MAP

Top: Moon over Wingate cliffs along Gunnison River. Bottom: Cottonwoods along Gunnison River north of Tunnell Point.

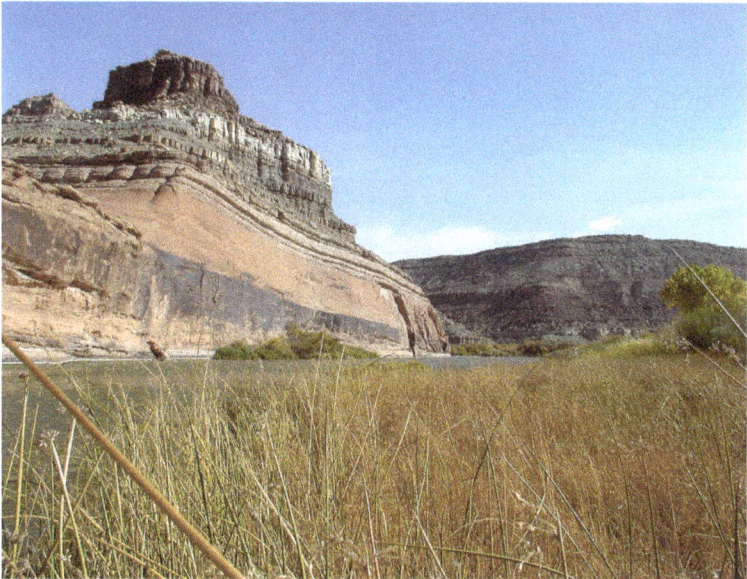

Top: "Rooster" Barnhart, BLM River Ranger, guide on the October 2017 river trip at Tunnel Point on Gunnison River. Bottom: Gunnison River where it loops around Tunnel Point.

Top: Lower section of Big Dominguez canyon with old livestock fencing.
Bottom: Escalante Canyon from rim of Cactus Flat west of Delta.

Top: Desert bighorn sheep in Escalante Canyon. Bottom: Along the Gunnison River on the trail to Big Dominguez canyon.

Top: Big Dominguez Campground and trailhead east into Big Dominguez Canyon. Bottom: Hikers on the trail up Big Dominguez Canyon.

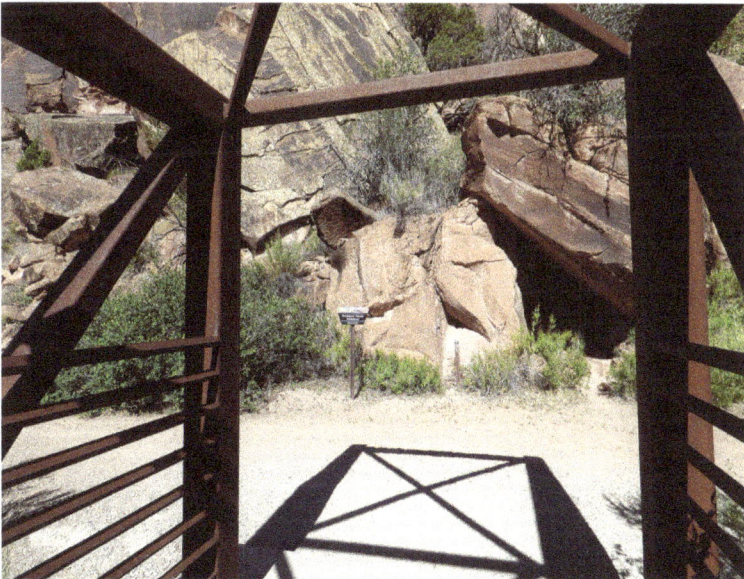

Top: Road at Escalante Forks looking east with Wingate cliffs. Bottom: West end of BLM public hiking bridge across Gunnison River and edge of Wilderness boundary.

Top: Becca Dykes, BLM wilderness ranger and author in Big Dominguez Canyon. Bottom: Big Dominguez creek before it goes over falls. Ancient bedrock over one billion years old.

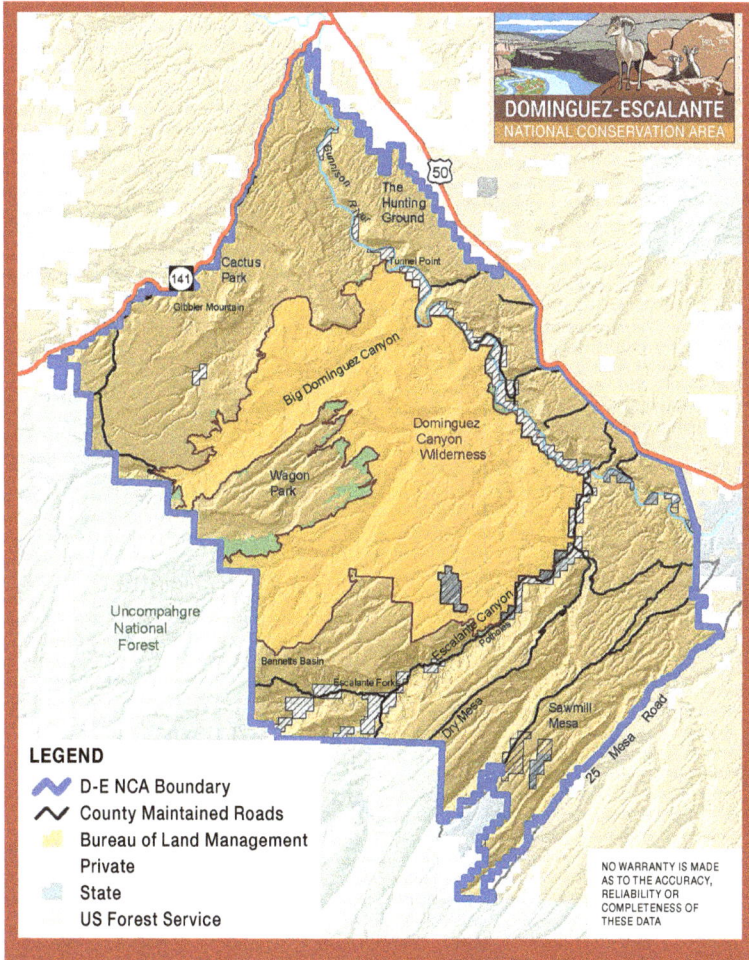

DOMINGUEZ-ESCALANTE
NATIONAL CONSERVATION AREA

LEGEND
- D-E NCA Boundary
- County Maintained Roads
- Bureau of Land Management
- Private
- State
- US Forest Service

NO WARRANTY IS MADE
AS TO THE ACCURACY,
RELIABILITY OR
COMPLETENESS OF
THESE DATA

Joseph is currently working on another book of reflections and meditations about the canyon country of western Colorado, including the Gunnison Gorge National Conservation Area adjacent to Black Canyon of the Gunnison National Park. The following is a preview of an essay from that collection.

EAGLE ROCK: WINTER SOLSTICE

I wonder if the ground has anything to say?
I wonder if the ground is listening to what is said?
Young Chief

I STOPPED AT THE edge of the cliff line as the trail wound on down below me. It was steep and whoever built the trail had placed several large flat rocks as stepping stones to get down the small cliff. I hesitated before stepping down, then stared out at the expansive view before and below me.

The clouds were low, hanging like grey sheets draping the sky, hiding the hills to the south. Light snow showers were whirling white dots in front of my eyes. The river wound through willow bottoms, hinting at its wandering and distant origin. The only sound was the soothing and timeless flow of the river.

That timeless view was what I came here to see. History. Not the history of the very rocks and hills, which usually absorb my attention on this edge of the Colorado Plateau. Instead, I was looking for history of early humans. The site is called Eagle Rock and I had heard news a few years ago that evidence had been unearthed of human habitation along the river dating back to 13,000 years. Plus or minus. But I had never visited the site. Now was the day. The weather added to the mystery and suspense. A storm was coming in from the southwest, as many storms do. These cliffs faced the southern horizon, which made me wonder at the wisdom of these people. The shelter had better be good, I thought. Otherwise, I hope these people were used to wind and snow blowing in their faces. On clear winter days, however, they would feel the welcome warmth of the sun.

This river gorge sits on the edge of the Colorado Rockies to the east. From here to the rising sun, mountain ridge upon ridge rise higher and higher. Thousands of years ago, that view would have been of glacial white erupting with roiling rivers of meltwater. There would be no habitation up there. To the west, the uplands of the Uncompahgre might have held a similar ice cap, as did the San Juan Mountains to the south. This river, gathering meltwaters from ice-capped mountains in all directions, flowed north then west again, to the slickrock canyons of Utah and Arizona that once was home to relatives of the people who lived here. The river was the only path of travel open to them.

Today, my travel was only a few hundred yards downhill to the cliff overhang. The significant journey for me today was only in my mind as I tried to understand what it would have been like to live here thirteen thousand summers earlier. More difficult to comprehend was the thirteen thousand December solstices. Just yesterday, the sun slowed to a stop and started its long journey back to green and summer heat, months away. The travel of the sun would have been what those people thought about. Would they have understood it wasn't the sun that moved, but this very earth that rotated in the heavens?

Did those ancients measure this sun journey like their descendants do? There are countless sites in this desert country with rock piles and notches that are prehistoric calendars. Would this site measure that? Or did these early people care beyond finding food and a better shelter from the snows and winds?

I climbed on down the rock steps and hiked the trail to the lower cliffs, just above the river bottom. I noticed the change from angular sandstone slabs to rounded rocks. River rocks. The river winding peacefully below me today once came up to this level and dropped the weathered and smoothed rocks it had carried for miles to this ancient shoreline. They are not sandstone, nor even the basalt from the nearby volcanic mountains of Grand Mesa or the West Elks. They came from miles away, carried by a torrent of glacial meltwater that had sculpted the higher granitic Rockies.

As I rounded the last curve of the trail, winding below an insignificant sandstone cliff face, I saw the wood rail fence that protects the site. Wheelbarrows and plastic buckets indicated the work still in progress but either halted for the holidays or probably the winter season. Interpretive signs, a surprise to me out here in what seems like a distant nowhere, tell the basic story. Look above on the cliff-face for the fading pictographs, or petroglyphs. They tell stories from the time long ago up until the recent times of Utes riding horses. The excavations dug deeply to the base of the cliff. More might be hidden under soil and rock blown in and fallen down. Had they found human bones? I had not done research prior to coming here, so I stood in ignorance. Sometimes, I don't want to know too many details.

I stared at the figures painted and carved on the rock. Faded, barely recognizable, but evident. Someone had stood here millennia ago writing to their gods or whomever they wanted to tell a story to. What were they saying? I had seen rock art before, but never this old. Who had lived here and what was their life like? Why did they choose this overhang, which to me seemed very exposed and inconsequential? Did they farm the river bottom? One of my companions this day had read up on the history and said the archaeologists had found little evidence of animal bones in the buried hearths of long ago. Were these early vegetarians? Surely they hunted meat. Was this just a quick stop on their travels or was it a permanent home?

As usually happens, I was full of questions that no one on earth could ever hope to answer with confidence. There were only guesses. This was a time so far beyond our ability to penetrate, we were strangers with no hope of finding answers.

I stood silently looking at the cliff face, then turned to face the river, not very far below. I wandered down a short section of wooden steps that had been recently built to access the water. Why were these here? Maybe the researchers needed water to wash off rocks and their digging. Or the route they brought in supplies, from the river itself. The shallow water from the ponds and sloughs of the nearby river was frozen solid. The river itself would rarely freeze, but it was several hundred yards away today. What was it like thirteen millennia ago? It may have washed right up against these cliffs.

The passage of time and the changes it brings have always intrigued me, especially in canyon country lined by sandstone cliffs. I let myself wander into the hanging clouds, seeing past the blowing snow, now getting heavier. I wanted to talk to these people. I tried. I closed my eyes and listened to the breeze. I heard the snowflakes hit my face, I felt the breeze carry away the sounds of the children playing here among the rocks while their parents scratched bighorn sheep figures on the rock cliff. I heard the women splashing water as they carried it in tightly woven reed baskets. An old man of thirty-five years sat hunched over fashioning a digging hoe from a piece of mottled granite.

I mentally stepped aside as a wolf-dog bounded past me to chase a rabbit that disappeared into the willows. There were no sounds that would indicate what I was familiar with in my present world. The sky, hidden now by lowering clouds, would be crossed by no jet contrails; no distant horn of passing coal trains would break the silence.

Try as I did, I could not put myself in that time in this place. It was a world that I inherited but I was a total stranger in. I felt a shiver. It was not the wind. It was a passing spirit who belonged here, coming into the future to speak to a stranger who inhabits a world he could not fathom either. He and I lived and breathed and looked similar but could never even talk to each other. People once lived here and I had come into their world. But an impenetrable barrier separates us.

Did a young boy stand here and pretend he had visited the future, seeing changes that were magic to his world? He would have looked across the river and seen a fruit orchard laid out in rows, overlooked by tall wind machines that stir the cold air on spring mornings. That would have been as foreign to him as his rock paintings are to me. Maybe the strange things he wondered about my world would have been my attempt to talk to my gods, influence my well-being. He would have marveled at the hard-soled boots that protect my feet from the sharp rocks. But he could not have understood the cell phone that my current day companion pulled out to check the weather forecast before leaving to drive back across the Continental Divide to his home on the Front Range. My silent companion from long ago could not understand mountains without glaciers much less such things as highways and automobiles with GPS mapping.

I was looking across a barrier thousands of years and worlds different from those people who once lived here. I could not touch that young boy nor could he touch me. We would have seen magic and mystery in each other.

I looked one final time at this shelter, this place of mystery that was slowly giving up secrets. But I knew there were some secrets it will hold forever. I started my slow climb back uphill, walking through time, back to a world I felt more comfortable in. A world I inherited from men and women and children who once walked this ground but who would forever keep their world apart from mine. People come and go, live and die. Life itself is the miracle we look for at this dark time of the year.

ABOUT THE AUTHOR

Joseph Colwell has worked and lived across the west for more than fifty years. During his college years at the University of Idaho, he spent summers working in Idaho state parks, Mt. Rainier National Park, and Grand Canyon National Park. With his degree in wildlife management, he spent the next twenty-seven years with the US Forest Service, working on five different national forests. Retiring from his Forest Service career, he continued work on wildland fires as a fire information officer, assisting the general public and homeowners in understanding wildfires.

He has authored two books of nature essays: *Canyon Breezes: Exploring Magical Places in Nature,* and *Zephyr of Time: Meditations on Time and Nature.* Both were published by Lichen Rock Press. In 2018 he published two books of fiction: *Sands of Time: A Flight of Discovery and Search for Meanings of Time,* and *Tales of Ravens Nest: A Life, A Place—Stories and Reflections.*

Joseph and his artist wife, Katherine, now live on their forty-acre nature preserve overlooking the North Fork Gunnison River Valley of western Colorado. They created Colwell Cedars Retreat, which offers a peaceful secluded haven for guests as well as wildlife. It is also a great place for thinking about geologic time. They can be reached at ColwellCedars.com

Colorado Canyons Association

A friend to the National Conservation Areas (NCAs), Colorado Canyons Association (CCA) is a nonpartisan, nonprofit volunteer organization that fosters community stewardship of the three NCAs in western Colorado through educational programs, events, and special partnerships.

CCA is the winner of BLM's 2016-2017 Public Lands Partnership Excellence Award.

You can be a friend, too. Donate, volunteer or join CCA in your next adventure through western Colorado NCAs. More information, events and opportunities can be found at ColoradoCanyonsAssociation.com

www.ingramcontent.com/pod-product-compliance
Lightning Source LLC
Chambersburg PA
CBHW041215030426
42336CB00023B/3354